Companioning You!

Also by Alan D. Wolfelt, Ph.D.

Companioning the Bereaved:
A Soulful Guide for Caregivers

Companioning the Dying: A Soulful Guide for Caregivers
by Greg Yoder   Foreword by Alan D. Wolfelt, Ph.D.

Companioning the Grieving Child:
A Soulful Guide for Caregivers

Companioning at a Time of Perinatal Loss: A Guide for Nurses, Physicians,
Social Workers and Chaplains in the Hospital Setting
by Jane Heustis & Marcia Meyer Jenkins   Foreword by Alan D. Wolfelt, Ph.D.

Understanding Your Grief: Ten Essential Touchstones
for Finding Hope and Healing Your Heart

Loving from the Outside In, Mourning from the Inside Out

Eight Critical Questions for Mourners: And the
Answers That Will Help You Heal

Companion Press is dedicated to the education and support of both the bereaved and
bereavement caregivers. We believe that those who companion the bereaved by walking
with them as they journey in grief have a wondrous opportunity: to help others
embrace and grow through grief—and to lead fuller, more deeply-lived lives themselves
because of this important ministry.

For a complete catalog and ordering information,
write or call or visit our website:

Companion
PRESS

Companion Press
The Center for Loss and Life Transition
3735 Broken Bow Road
Fort Collins, CO 80526

(970) 226-6050   FAX 1-800-922-6051
drwolfelt@centerforloss.com www.centerforloss.com

Companioning You!

A Soulful Guide to Caring for Yourself
While You Care for the Dying and the Bereaved

Alan D. Wolfelt, Ph.D.

Companion Press is an imprint of the Center for Loss and Life Transition, 3735 Broken Bow Road, Fort Collins, Colorado 80526, (970) 226-6050, www.centerforloss.com.

Companion Press books may be purchased in bulk for sales promotions, premiums and fundraisers. Please contact the publisher at the above address for more information.

Printed in the United States of America.

23 22 21 20 19 18 17 16   5 4 3 2

ISBN 978-1-61722-166-8

To the thousands of caregivers who have traveled to Colorado to train with me in the "companioning" principles of caring for the dying and the bereaved. Your willingness to inspire me to teach about caring for ourselves as we care for the dying and the bereaved has given birth to this resource. Thank you so much for your support of my body of work in death education and counseling.

Companion Press is dedicated to the education and support of both the bereaved and bereavement caregivers. We believe that those who companion the bereaved by walking with them as they journey in grief have a wondrous opportunity: to help others embrace and grow through grief—and to lead fuller, more deeply-lived lives themselves because of this important ministry.

For a complete catalog and ordering information,

write or call or visit our website:

Companion
PRESS

Companion Press
The Center for Loss and Life Transition
3735 Broken Bow Road
Fort Collins, CO 80526
(970) 226-6050
FAX 1-800-922-6051
drwolfelt@centerforloss.com
www.centerforloss.com

Contents

If Someone Gave You This Book 1

Introduction 3

Part One —
Understanding Your Own Companioning Philosophy and Style 9
  My Companioning Philosophy 11
    My Personal Tenets of Companioning the Bereaved 15
  Embracing the Importance of Companioning You 22
  Exploring Your Personal Loss Background, Current Issues,
    and Motivations 25
  Zen and the Art of Erasing Worktapes 34
  Understanding Caregiver Burnout 39
  The Spillover Effects of Burnout 45
  Emotional Involvement and Stress 47
  The Overcaring Caregiver 49
  The Perfectionistic Caregiver 53

Part Two —
An Eight-Week Self-Companioning Makeover for
Caregivers to the Dying and the Bereaved 59
  Before You Begin 61
  Week 1: Acknowledge the Reality of Any Imbalance and
    Surrender to It 64
  Week 2: Inventory Any Hurts and Unhappiness You Are Experiencing .. 69
  Week 3: Create a Vision for Moving Forward and Set Your Intention 75
  Week 4: Set Aside Time *Each And Every Day From Now On* To
    Touch Base With Your Spirit 82
  Week 5: Rebalance Your Daily Habits and Schedule 88
  Week 6: Carve Out *More* Sacred Downtime—
    Weekly, Monthly, Yearly 95
  Week 7: Seek Joy 101
  Week 8: Revise 107

A Final Word 111

A Self-Companionship Manifesto for Caregivers to the
  Dying and the Bereaved 113

If Someone Gave You This Book

The person or organization that gave you this book cares about you and wants the very best for you. They understand that caring for the dying and the bereaved is a naturally stressful experience. It is given to you as a gift along with the hope and prayer that it will help you care as much for yourself as you do for others. Please accept it in that spirit, and let others who companion their fellow human beings during times of grief and loss know about it as well.

Someone very wise once observed, "A good book is the best of friends, the same today and forever." My hope is that this resource becomes a friend to you and helps you embrace the critical importance of self-companionship as you continue to companion others.

Alan D. Wolfelt

Introduction

I feel so honored to write, teach, and counsel about death, dying, grief, and loss. Like you, I am proud of (yet continually humbled by) the work I do with dying and grieving people. Yet I also recognize that with my work comes an obligation to take excellent care of myself, because without good self-care, I can't be truly present to the fellow human beings I companion. As the saying goes, "You can never take anyone any further than you go yourself."

✳✳✳✳✳✳✳✳✳✳

Companioning versus taking care of

To "companion" the dying and the bereaved means to be an active participant in their grief journeys. When you companion the dying and the bereaved instead of "taking care of them," you allow yourself to learn from their unique experiences. You let them teach you instead of the other way around.

✳✳✳✳✳✳✳✳✳✳

Herein lies the critical caregiver conundrum: How do you companion yourself while at the same time companioning others? The title of this book is *Companioning You*, and by this I mean that it is essential to give yourself the same focused, compassionate, you-centric companionship that you give your clients.

If you are reading this, you may be a hospice staff member, clergyperson, social worker, chaplain, nurse, grief counselor, physician, or volunteer. (Trust that if you are reading this, you are *supposed* to be reading it!) Whatever your specific caregiving role, I welcome you. Perhaps like me, you are aware that you may be good at meeting the needs of everyone else but tend to ignore or minimize your own needs. If so, this resource should be of help to you.

Here at the Center for Loss and Life Transition in Colorado, where I serve as Director, many levels of decks and two sacred gazebos connect the redwood pathways that meander the steep, rugged terrain. Nestled as they are among the pines, these tranquil seating areas—overlooking the city of Fort Collins to the east and the breathtakingly beautiful Rocky Mountains to the west—invite relaxation and quiet meditation. Simply walk by the gazebos and you are pulled, like a magnet, into their restorative purview.

But I must confess that I, like many caregivers, resisted their pull all too often. It has only been in recent years that I have acknowledged my need for conscious self-companionship and have worked to create more balance in my life. Here I was, living and working in this incredible environment yet spending little time really enjoying it. I was focusing on doing, and helping others, instead of being, and helping myself.

In my thirty years as a caregiver, the world has seemed to move faster and faster, and become progressively busier and more complicated. In these days of post-September 11, 2001, we are a worried and anxious culture. Approximately one out of three people in our general population complains about sleep disturbance and exhaustion. Many people are depressed or suffer from anxiety disorders. Seventy to ninety percent of visits to primary care physicians are attributed to stress. Yet you choose to companion the dying and the bereaved? Bless your soul!

In his bestselling book *Margin: Restoring Emotional, Physical, Financial, and Time Reserves to Overloaded Lives*, physician-futurist Dr. Richard A. Swenson explores the idea that we as a culture used to allow spare time. But in today's marginless existence, we schedule our demands back-to-back-to-back, with no room to make a mistake or even take a breath. "Margin is the space between our load and our limits and is related to our reserves and resilience," he writes. "It is a buffer, a leeway, a gap; the place we go to heal, to relate, to reflect, to recharge our batteries, to focus on the things that matter most." Without margin, we struggle and stress.

The good news is that you don't have to become a statistic. However, to stay balanced in an unbalanced world takes discernment and common sense. Without doubt, every day you have a choice to practice stress or to practice peace. We can be caregivers who love what we do, who love helping others, yet who also remember to care for ourselves at the same time. I appreciate that you are making this book a priority right now. Put your "to do" list aside for the moment. (Rest assured, it will outlive you.)

Why is this book subtitled a "soulful guide"? When people have come to me for support in grief, the soul is present. When they try as best they can to wrap words around their grief, trusting me with their vulnerability, I know we are meeting at a soul level. To look into the eyes of someone mourning the death of someone precious is to peer into the window of the soul. Likewise, truly seeking to understand and embrace the art of self-companionship is a journey of revealing and connecting with your own soul. To companion yourself is to look with compassion, yet pure honesty, at your own soul and to nurture the divine spark you find there.

I have filled the following pages with concise, practical information intended to help you practice ongoing, compassionate self-companionship. This book is intentionally a quick read. After all, if I make it too long, many of you caregivers won't make time to read and ponder it! The self-companionship makeover in Part 2 contains a process and practical tips for you to consider as you live your personal and caregiving lives with purpose, conviction, courage, hope, faith, kindness, wisdom, and peace.

I suggest that the most effective way to use this book is to read it all the way through once, from beginning to end. Then, once you've immersed yourself in the concepts and have an understanding of the makeover process, I invite you to actually work through the eight-week makeover. Those of you who choose not to step through the entire makeover process may still find it contains helpful insights and activities. Down the road, whenever you become aware that your commitment to self-companionship may be flagging, I urge you to reread this entire book and reengage in the makeover to reinvigorate your commitment to excellent self-companionship.

Companioning yourself is even more enjoyable if you share your intentions and progress with someone else. Throughout the book I mention that you should have and rely on a "responsibility partner." I strongly encourage you to read this book at the same time as your partner and then step through the eight-week makeover process together. Or, form a

"Companioning You Discernment Group" with some of your colleagues and use this resource as your workbook to help you achieve balance, peace, and harmony in your life. If you take the contents of this book to heart and put them into action, the changes you will experience are likely to amaze and surprise you. All you have to do is turn the page…

Part One

Understanding Your Own Companioning Philosophy and Style

My Companioning Philosophy

Before we continue on with our conversation about the whys and hows of self-companionship for caregivers to the dying and the bereaved, I'd like to take a step backward to reiterate my basic companioning philosophy. After all, if you're not clear about what I mean by companioning others, how can you understand and embrace companioning yourself, for heaven's sake? (If, on the other hand, you're already a companioning insider and advocate, you may want to skip ahead to the next section.)

I've always found it intriguing that the word "treat" comes from the Latin root word *tractare*, which means "to drag." If we combine that with "patient," we can really get in trouble. "Patient" means "passive long-term sufferer," so if we treat patients, we drag passive, long-term sufferers. Simply stated, that's not very empowering to me.

On the other hand, the word "companion," when broken down into its original Latin roots, means "messmate": *com* for "with" and *pan* for "bread." Someone you would share a meal with, a friend, an equal. I have taken liberties with the noun "companion" and made it into the verb "companioning" because it so well captures the type of counseling relationship I support and advocate. In fact, that is the very image of companioning—sitting at a table together, being present to one another, sharing, communing, abiding in the fellowship of hospitality.

Companioning the dying and the bereaved is therefore not about assessing, analyzing, fixing, or resolving another's grief. Instead, it is about being totally present to the mourner—even being a temporary guardian of her soul.

The companioning model is anchored in a "teach-me" perspective. It is about learning and observing. In fact, the meaning of "observance" comes to us from ritual. It means not only to "watch out for" but also "to keep and honor," "to bear witness." The caregiver's awareness of this need to learn is the essence of true companioning.

If your desire is to support a fellow human in grief, you must create a "safe place" for people to embrace their feelings of profound loss. This safe place is a cleaned-out, compassionate heart. It is the open heart that allows you to be truly present to another human being's intimate pain. (Yet it is this same open heart that puts you at risk for compassion fatigue.)

As a caregiver to the dying and the bereaved, I am a companion, not a "guide"—which assumes a knowledge of another's soul I cannot claim. To companion our fellow humans means to watch and learn. Our awareness of the need to learn (as opposed to our tendency to play the expert) is the essence of true companioning.

A central role of the companion to a mourner is related to the art of honoring stories. Honoring stories requires that we slow down, turn inward, and really listen as people acknowledge the reality of loss, embrace pain, review memories, and search for meaning.

The philosophy and practice of companioning also inter-faces naturally with the art of hospitality. Hospitality is the essence of knowing how to live in society. Among the ancient Greeks, hospitality was a necessary element of day-to-day life. In a land where borders were permeable, it was important to get to know one's neighbors as potential friends. One way to do this was to share meals together. First, the guest and host would pour a libation to the gods. Then they would eat ("break bread") together. Then, after the guest was full, they would tell each other their stories, with the guest going first. Often, tears were shed because their stories were highly personal; battles, family, histories, and life tragedies were retold. After the evening together, the host and guest were potential allies. Still today, breaking bread and sharing personal stories are key elements of companioning people through death and grief.

Henri Nouwen once elegantly described hospitality as the "creation of a free space where the stranger can enter and become a friend instead of an enemy." He observed that hospitality is not about trying to change people, but instead about offering them space where change can take place. He astutely noted, "Hospitality is not a subtle invitation to adopt the lifestyle of the host, but the gift of a chance for the guest to find his own."

Also interesting to note is that the *Oxford English Dictionary* defines companion as "to accompany, to associate, to comfort, to be familiar with." This definition is actually illustrative of what it means to companion. In one sense, the notion is of comforting someone, which relates clearly to what the dying and the bereaved need and deserve. In another sense, the notion is of knowing someone, of being familiar with that person's experiences

"As a hospice grief counselor and intern supervisor, I sit with clients every day who have lost a loved one, as well as listen to the client stories the interns share with me. There is no way I can carry all the pain shared within the walls of my office. Besides my faith, my saving grace and what keeps me sane and returning to work each day is Dr. Wolfelt's companioning model of grief counseling. I remind myself daily that it is not my job to take away my client's pain. It is their journey, not mine. I need only be present to witness their pain, to companion them on their journey, to walk alongside them, not in their shoes. Oh, I take vacations and I travel and I spend as much time with my grandchildren as possible. All of those things refresh and energize me. But at the end of the day, and at the beginning, it is knowing that I am not responsible for taking away anyone's pain, knowing that I need only to be present as a companion, that is most helpful for me. I express gratitude every day for the privilege of doing this 'heart and soul' work. I am truly blessed."

— Laura Larson, LCSW

and needs. This clearly relates to the process of becoming familiar (being open to being taught by another), which can take place through the "telling of the story."

In sum, companioning is the art of bringing comfort and bearing witness to another by becoming familiar with her story (experiences and needs). To companion the grieving and the dying, therefore, is to break bread literally or figuratively, and to listen to the story of the other. Of course this may well involve tears and sorrow, and tends toward give-and-take: I tell you my story and you tell me yours. It is sharing in a deep and profound way.

My Personal Tenets of Companioning the Bereaved

I believe that every caregiver must work to develop his or her own theory or point of view about what helps the dying and the bereaved. Challenging yourself to explain what happens in your caregiving relationships with dying and grieving people and families will, in my experience, assist you in understanding and improving the results of the work you do to assist those you desire to companion.

Developing your own tenets encourages a coherence of ideas about the helping process and also generates new ideas about how to be helpful. Outlined below are 20 principles that undergird *my* work. My hope is that you will challenge yourself to write out your philosophy of effective caregiving to the dying and the bereaved.

For the Companion to the Dying and the Bereaved:

1. Bereavement, grief, and mourning are normal and necessary experiences; however, they are often traumatic and transformative.

2. The helping process is seen as a collaborative, "companioning" process among people. The traditional medical model of mental health care is inadequate and complicating. As a companion, I try to create conditions that engage people actively in the reconciliation needs of mourning.

3. True expertise in grief or death lies with (and only with) the unique person who is grieving or dying. Only he can be the expert. The companion is there to learn from the griever and to bear witness to and normalize his journey.

4. The foundation upon which helping the bereaved or the dying person takes place is in the context of an encouraging, hope-filled relationship between the counselor and the client. The widely acknowledged core conditions of helping (empathy, warmth and caring, genuineness, respect) are seen as essential ingredients in working with bereaved and dying people and families.

5. Traditional mental health diagnostic categories are seen as limitations on the helping process. The concept of "gardening" as opposed to "assessing" better describes efforts to understand the meaning of the journey in the dying or bereaved person's life. I strive to understand not only the potential complications of the

journey, but also individual strengths and levels of wellness.

6. The counseling model is holistic in nature and views bereaved and dying people as physical, emotional, cognitive, social, and spiritual beings. Each person is unique and seeks not just to "be," but to become.

7. The underlying theoretical model is systems-oriented and sees the bereaved or dying person as being a node in a web of interdependent relationships with society and other people, groups, and institutions.

8. The focus of companioning the bereaved or dying person is balanced between the past, the present, and the future. Learning about past life experiences (particularly family of origin influences) and the nature of important relationships between the client and the important people in her life help me understand the meaning of the dying, grief, and mourning process for this unique person.

9. A dying or bereaved person's perception of her reality is her reality. A "here and now" understanding of that reality allows me to be with her where she is instead of trying to push her somewhere she is not. I will be a more effective helper if I remember to enter into a person's feelings without having a need to change her feelings.

10. A major helping goal is to provide a "safe place" for the dying or bereaved person to do the work of mourning, resulting in healing and growth. The dying or bereaved person does not have an illness I need to cure. I'm a caregiver, not a cure-giver!

11. People are viewed from a multicultural perspective. What is considered "normal" in one culture may be perceived as "abnormal" in another culture. On a shrinking planet, my caring and concern must be global in its perspective.

12. Spiritual and religious concerns and needs are seen as central to the reconciliation process. To be an effective counselor, I must be tuned in to helping people grow in depth and vitality in their spiritual and religious lives as they search for meaning and purpose in their continued living.

13. Men and women are seen in androgynous ways that encourage understanding beyond traditional sex-role stereotypes. Artful companions understand that bonded relationships exist outside the boundaries of traditional male-female partnerships and marriage.

14. The overall goal of helping the dying and the bereaved is reconciliation, not resolution. As a companion, I have a responsibility not to help the dying or bereaved person return to an "old normal," but instead to discover how death and dying change him in many different ways. Traditional mental health models that teach resolution as the helping goal are seen as self-limiting and potentially destructive to the dying or bereaved person.

15. Right-brain methods of healing and growth (intuitive, metaphoric) are seen as valuable and are integrated with left-brain methods (intentional, problem-solving approaches). This synergy encourages a more growth-filled approach to death and bereavement caregiving

than do historical mental health models (primarily based on left-brain methods) of caregiving.

16. "Complicated" mourning is perceived as blocked growth. The "complicated mourner" probably simply needs help in understanding the central needs of mourning and how to embrace them in ways that help him heal. Most people are where they are in their grief journeys for one of two major reasons: 1) That is where they need to be at this point in their journey; or, 2) They need, yet lack, an understanding, safe place for mourning and a person who can help facilitate their work of mourning in more growth-producing, hope-filled ways.

17. Helping avenues must be adapted to the unique needs of the dying or bereaved person. Some people are responsive to group work, some to individual work, and some to family systems work. Many people are best served, in fact, by seeking support from lay companions who have walked before them in the grief journey.

18. There is a commitment to using educational, primary prevention efforts to impact societal change because we live in a "mourning-avoiding" culture. I have a responsibility to inform other people throughout the world of the need to create safe places for people to mourn in healthy ways.

19. There is a responsibility to create conditions for healing to take place in the bereaved person. The ultimate responsibility for eventual healing lies within

"I've learned lots about myself as a caregiver. When I first started, I let it consume me. As I've grown and learned from courses, the dying person, families, and other individuals, each situation is different. I've learned that I'm not in control when someone will die. They choose when they will go, or our higher power, depending on your belief system, will make that decision. I at first thought that every person should have someone with them so as not to be alone when they die. But I've seen many times when a person has waited until everyone or certain people have left in order to die the way they want to. I've also learned to look after myself by exercising, eating properly, and just getting away from all of it. Even if it's just to play a guitar or read a book, sometimes you need to remember you are alive and you are still here, needed by family and friends, even though you don't forget what is happening with your patients. Sometimes stepping back is hard to do, but I've been in situations where stepping back is the best thing. People need to grieve and deal with things in their own way."

— Lorie Parsons

the person. I must remember to be responsible *to* dying and bereaved people, not responsible *for* them.

20. Excellent self-care is essential, for it provides the physical, spiritual, emotional, social, and cognitive renewal necessary for the caregiver to be an effective, ongoing companion in grief.

So that is what I mean by companioning (versus taking care of) the dying and the bereaved. The remainder of this book explores how to take this companioning lens and turn it on yourself in ways that bring you energy, joy, love, and a sense of peace—not only in your work with the dying and the bereaved but in every moment you breathe. For companioning others is indeed rewarding and honorable work, but if you are not at the same time companioning yourself, your life will be out of balance and you will likely be both unhappy and ineffective in your work as well as your personal life.

Embracing the Importance of Companioning You

For caregivers to the dying and the bereaved, good self-companionship is critical for at least three major reasons.

First and most important, we owe it to ourselves and our families to lead joyful, whole lives. While companioning the dying and the bereaved is certainly rewarding, we cannot and should not expect our work to fulfill us completely.

Second, our work is draining—physically, emotionally, and spiritually. Assisting bereaved and dying people is a demanding interpersonal process that requires much energy and focus. Whenever we attempt to respond to the needs of those in grief, chances are slim that we can (or should) avoid the stress of emotional involvement. Each day we open ourselves to caring about the dying and the bereaved and their personal life journeys. And genuinely caring about people and their families touches the depths of our hearts and souls. We need relief from such draining work.

And third, we owe it to our clients themselves. My personal experience and observation suggest that good self-companionship is an essential foundation of caring about the dying and the bereaved. They are sensitive to our ability to "be with" them. Poor self-care results in distraction from the helping relationship, and dying and bereaved people often intuit when we are not physically, emotionally, and spiritually available to them.

Sometimes caregivers who practice poor self-companionship also distance themselves from others' pain by taking on the stance of the "expert." Because many of us have been trained to remain professionally distant, we may stay aloof from the very people we are supposed to help. Generally, this is a projection of our own need to stay removed from the pain of others as well as from our own life hurts. Yet the expert mode is antithetical to compassionate care, and can cause an irreparable rift between you and those you are honored to companion.

So, does this work have to be exhausting? Naturally, draining, yes, but exhausting? I don't think so. Yes, good helpers naturally focus outward, resulting in a drain on both head and heart. And yes, you will hear some people say, "If you do this kind of caregiving, you might as well resign yourself to eventually burning out." Again, I don't think so. I have been doing it for over three decades and can honestly say I feel so blessed to do what I do to help my fellow human beings each and every day. I hope you can say the same.

The key to burnout prevention is to practice daily, ongoing, nurturing self-companionship. If you are not already doing so, you may simply need to try on some new ways of thinking and being.

"Early in my work with people, I noted how imperative it is to 'take care of the instrument of care'... myself. I realized how being tired or overstressed affects my ability to pay attention to the person across from me telling me their story, or how my tolerance for challenging behaviors with others would vary depending on my own state of being. I am a fan of saying 'you cheat folks out of 25 percent of you if you are only functioning at 75 percent most days.' Since I am the instrument of care, I know it is in my example of self-care that I model good self-care for others. I see good self-care as a responsibility as much as a need. I regularly assess my needs for exercise, for unplugging and getting into nature, for eating well, for playing and being silly, and for resting. All of these greatly impact my ability to be my best with others. I feel I owe people my 100 percent. People benefit most from my full attention, listening, and cognitive abilities as I navigate alongside them. People who come across our paths deserve our best."

— Amy L. Kitsembel

Exploring Your Personal Loss Background, Current Issues, and Motivations

To companion your fellow human beings during times of grief and loss, you must stay very self-aware of your own issues. Working in this area of caregiving puts you face-to-face with your own fears of losing people close to you and of facing your own mortality.

Allow me to provide a framework for you to explore three important areas of loss self-awareness:

1. Your Background Related to Death and Life Losses;
2. Your Current Personal Issues Surrounding Grief and Loss; and
3. Your Motivations as a Caregiver.

Your Background Related to Death and Life Losses

As caregivers we come from all sorts of different backgrounds and life experiences. Each of us comes from our own unique family of origin and cultural context. Some of us have a history of loss (it is true that your greatest gifts often come from your wounds), while others do not. Some of the families we were raised in were open and honest about death and grief, while others tried to deny or go around grief instead of through it.

To enhance your awareness of your experiences with grief and loss and the ways in which your attitudes have been shaped, please explore the following questions:

- What was your first experience with death? What thoughts and feelings did you have at that time?

- How did your family, friends, and other significant people in your life respond at that time?
- What do you recall as you reflect backward on this experience?
- How were death and grief handled in your family of origin?
- Were they discussed openly and honestly?
- Were they considered taboo topics?
- How did your family's treatment of death and grief impact you?
- Do you recall experiencing the death of companion animals in your family? What was that like for you? Was your family supportive of your need to mourn?
- What experiences with funerals have you had?
- If the first funeral you experienced was as a child, were you nurtured by adults around you? Did you feel a sense of inclusion or exclusion from funeral experiences as a child?
- What childhood experiences did you have of being in the presence of dead bodies? What was that like for you?
- How did your family's religious, cultural, and ethnic background influence your experiences with death?
- What is your understanding of how your early experiences with death influenced your life?
- What other losses have you had in your life (divorce, moves, job loss, etc.)? Were you able to mourn these life transitions?
- Of the people in your life who are still alive, which ones' deaths would be the most difficult for you? Why do you think that is?
- When do you think it is appropriate to share your own loss experiences with grieving people you companion?

Your Current Personal Issues Surrounding Grief and Loss

As you companion your fellow human beings in loss, you naturally reflect on your own life losses. Your personal history of loss can help or, at times (if you yourself don't practice what you believe about the need to mourn), hinder your caregiving efforts. As I've said, we can never take anyone any further than we go ourselves. Therefore, we must always stay conscious of our own mourning needs.

When we experience losses in our own lives, it's time to step back and tend to our own grief. Obviously, there is no shame in seeking support and doing our own mourning. If we don't, there is a risk that we will project our own issues into the helping relationship and unconsciously try to meet our own needs for support and understanding. Be sure you have a "responsibility partner" who can help you discern where you are with your grief journeys.

Conversely, some people project that when we as caregivers experience life losses, we lose objectivity and are unable to assist others. I totally disagree! As long as we do our own grief work, the losses that touch our lives can actually heighten our empathy and result in greater depth of understanding. But a warning: Always be sure to separate your needs from the needs of those you have the honor of companioning.

"I am a medical social worker with a hospice for six years and have noticed some signs of burnout, such as extreme fatigue, anxiety, and loss of ability to concentrate. In the past year I have been on a quest to cope with this cumulative grief so I can continue this work that I love. In addition to biking, hiking, traveling, and taking a day off during the week, I have begun a journal of my thoughts and feelings about death and dying and my connections to my patients. It has also been very therapeutic to have a monthly bereavement session with all our staff—nurses, social workers, chaplain, and bereavement counselor—to discuss our feelings and losses with our patients (and in our own lives). I also try to attend funerals and viewings of the patients to have some closure and learn about their lives before they were sick. I also keep a copy of their obituary in my journal. I feel I must have some closure and experience my grief with each patient relationship before I can be open to the next one. I will often touch them and whisper a good-bye the last time I see them. I am trying to be "active" in my grief and in allowing myself to feel my feelings and make meaning out of the work I do and my relationships with other people."

— Camille Kennard, LCSW

Of course, the nature of our work does expose us to more loss than most people. In caring for the dying, for example, we naturally grow close to those we help. When they die, we come to grief and need to mourn. We must have the ongoing support to explore how these losses impact us, both personally and professionally. We are also at risk for "bereavement overload," where before we have mourned one loss, we might experience another. Again, ongoing support and the use of a "responsibility partner" is vital to good self-companionship. Don't be surprised if, from time to time, you need a mini-sabbatical away from death, dying, grief, and loss. There is no shame in taking this time away, only wise discernment!

Make use of the following questions to assist you in looking at your current personal loss issues:

- Which personal losses are currently influencing your life journey? What are you doing with these losses? Whom do you turn to for support surrounding these losses? Where do you see yourself in integrating these losses into your life?
- Who serves as your "responsibility partner"? How often do you see this person? How do you make use of your time together?
- Do you have any sense that you may project your own loss issues into the work you do to help others? If so, how so? If not, why not? What do you do to have clarity around "your" life issues versus "their" life issues?
- Have you ever experienced "loss overload"? If so, what have you done to acknowledge this and take care of yourself? How often are you able to go to exile and be away from death, dying, and grief?

Your Motivation As a Caregiver

My experience suggests that people go into this rewarding but stressful area of caregiving for a multitude of different reasons. Regardless of your unique motivations, I believe it is important to explore and understand them.

Caring for the dying and bereaved tends to draw people who care deeply about people, are highly motivated to help others, and are often idealistic, expecting this area of caregiving to give them a tremendous sense of meaning and purpose. This is particularly true of those who see this work as a "calling" (a concept I believe in and identify with myself, by the way, but a concept that can also put those of us who are called at risk of burnout).

Yes, I have seen firsthand that people who come into this area of work, who have entered with a strong desire to give of themselves to others—and actually felt helpful, excited, and idealistic during their early years as caregivers to the dying and the bereaved—are susceptible to burnout. People experience burnout as a gradual erosion of their spirit, "life force," and zest for life and work. I don't want this to happen to you. That is why this book stresses the importance of self-companionship.

Some caregivers enter into the profession wanting to "rescue" people from distress, pain, and suffering. Within medical institutions, death is often projected to be the "final enemy" to be fought. In contrast, hospice care is organized around the principle of helping people experience a "good death," which often implies a death this is pain-free and attended by significant others, takes place in a home-like setting, is influenced to some degree by patient and family choices, and brings "resolution" or "acceptance" to the life that is ending. This concept of a "good death" is also referred to as a "natural death," "appropriate death," or "death with dignity" in hospice literature.

Obviously, this goal of a "good death" can also be a source of stress, strain, and disappointment in situations where the ideal is not experienced. It is important that the "rescue" phenomenon and any romantic perception of always achieving a "good death" are explored and understood. Otherwise there can be disillusionment, disappointment, frustration, and a sense of failure.

Similarly, our understanding of what constitutes "healthy mourning"—and whether we've helped those in our care achieve it—can affect our feelings of success or failure as care-givers to the bereaved. While I am certainly an advocate for helping those in grief meet what I call the six needs of mourning (acknowledge the reality of the death; move toward the pain of the loss; remember the person who died; develop a new self-identity; search for meaning; and accept support from others), I am at risk for the same disillusionment, disap-pointment, frustration, and sense of failure if I believe myself responsible for these outcomes.

Effective self-companionship is rooted in understanding the normalcy of both of these phenomena.

Make use of the following questions to assist you in exploring your motivations as a caregiver to the dying and the bereaved:

- How would you describe your motivation to work in this area of caregiving? What is the most rewarding aspect of

※※※※※※※※※※※※※※※※※※※※※※※※

Burnout, compassion fatigue, or vicarious trauma?

Over the years, clinicians and academics have developed labels to describe and separate the various types of debility that can result from any work that requires a great deal of focused empathy.

The terms *burnout, compassion fatigue,* and *vicarious trauma* are three of the most-used labels, and they are applied not only to caregivers to the dying and the bereaved, but also to people whose work involves witnessing trauma (such as police officers and emergency room staff) or helping people who have been victimized (such as child protection workers), as well as those engaged in other forms of human services (such as social workers, addiction counselors, etc.).

Burnout is typically defined as emotional and physical exhaustion (also see Maslach's definition of burnout on pg. 42), while compassion fatigue is generally used to refer to cases in which empathy erosion is prominent. Vicarious trauma is generally reserved for times when the caregiver experiences a profound shift in worldview after working with clients who have suffered a trauma.

There are gray areas and overlaps among the three, of course, and they are not mutually exclusive. A caregiver who is feeling burned out may also be experiencing some degree of compassion fatigue, for example.

For purposes of this resource, I am not trying to help you decide which of the three (or what mixture) you might be experiencing. I am simply addressing the *general* category of burnout and will use the term "burnout" to represent it.

Note: If your symptoms are debilitating and might be considered clinical depression, post-traumatic stress, attachment disorder as a result of compassion fatigue, chemical abuse or addiction, or any other severe condition, I urge you to muster the self-regard to seek the help of a therapist or other professional. You deserve the same compassion you have shown so many others!

※※※※※※※※※※※※※※※※※※※※※※※※

what you do? What is the most stressful aspect of what you do?

- Does this work provide you with a sense of meaning and purpose? If so, why do you think that is?
- What has been your vocational path? How did you end up in this profession? What is your specific job description right now?
- What is it like for you when you are unable to help people experience a "good death" or "healthy mourning"?
- If you are a bereavement caregiver, what is it like for you when you realize that we, as humans, never really completely "resolve" grief? How do you know that you are making a real difference in the lives of those you companion?
- What do you think some of the different motivations are for people who enter into this area of caregiving?

I hope this self-exploration has provided you with a foundation for enhanced understanding of your background related to death and life losses, your current personal issues surrounding grief and loss, and your motivation as a caregiver. Now let's talk about some of the common work mythologies that many people in our culture share.

Zen and the Art of Erasing Worktapes

I'm reminded of the caregiver who goes to visit the wise Zen master. The Zen master instantly sees that the caregiver is rather set in his ways and gives to others at all cost to self. He decides to teach the caregiver a vital lesson.

The wise teacher picks up a pitcher of spring water and begins filling the caregiver's cup. He fills the cup and it overflows, spilling out over the edges and onto the floor.

"Teacher!" shouts the caregiver in shock. "Can't you see? My cup is already full. There is no room for more water in it!"

"Just the same as your mind," answers the teacher. "If you wish to have room for new ideas, first you must empty your head of the old ideas that are blocking your mind."

Caregivers to the dying and bereaved come in many varieties. You may be young or old; female or male; white or Hispanic or African-American; Democrat or Republican; Methodist, Baptist, Catholic, or atheist. But there is one thing you all have in common: You work very, very hard and you are very, very busy.

So why do death and grief caregivers seem particularly prone to workaholism? Many have been influenced by what I call "Caregiver Worktapes." These worktapes are mostly unconscious messages about work that are stored away in the recesses of your brain. It is as if your mind plays them over and over again, but at a level so deep that your conscious mind cannot easily articulate them. These messages, which you learn from your parents, from people you have worked for, and from colleagues, can program your work behavior in ways you may not even be aware of.

The problem with worktapes is that unless you learn to consciously hear them and to turn down the volume or turn them off completely when they threaten your well-being, they may drive you to exhaustion, frustration, and depression.

Outlined below are four common worktapes for caregivers to the dying and the bereaved. If you are honest with yourself, you may see yourself in at least some of them.

Worktape #1: Be Available at All Times

"If you really care, you must be available at all times," this worktape insists. True, there are time when being available is important and necessary. However, being *always* available leads to burnout and is not a good practice to get into.

Why? First, you have limitations, physically and emotionally. No one can sanely work morning, noon, and night AND have a home life. If your "Be Available at All Times" worktape forces you into this type of schedule, you run the risk of having so much energy directed outward that you lose touch with your inner self. Do you ever wonder, "Who is this stranger called 'me'?"

The second reason for turning off this worktape is that it dilutes your effectiveness. Focusing a little bit of yourself on everything means committing a great deal of yourself to nothing. The result can be *polyphasic behavior*, which means, at bottom, that you have a lot to do but feel like you are not accomplishing much.

This worktape also allows Parkinson's Law to take control of your life: your work will expand to fill the time available. Depression, divorce, physical problems, chemical abuse, and premature death are all too common among those who become slaves to this mythic worktape.

Worktape #2: If You're Resting, You're Lazy

"What are you doing sitting down? There is always something to do around here." Many people confuse constant activity with productivity. Sometimes managers reinforce this thinking because they find it hard to measure an employee's effectiveness. Therefore, activity replaces results as the measure of performance. The busiest bee is thought to be the best worker and is rewarded accordingly.

Yet, have you ever encountered people who look and act busy but never seem to accomplish much? Effectiveness must take precedence over busy-ness.

To maintain your physical and emotional health, you need to have downtime in which to pull back and recharge. If you don't allow yourself to rest, you will likely not only lose your enthusiasm for your work, you will also become exhausted and depressed. As poet e.e. cummings once noted, "If you can be, be. If not, cheer up and go on about other people's business, doing and undoing unto others 'til you drop."

Worktape #3: No Pain, No Gain

"We must go the extra mile." Referred to by some as the "buckets of sweat syndrome," this myth would have you believe that results are directly related to how hard you work.

This worktape can put you in the mode of constantly working hard to the exclusion of restorative times of rest, play, and relaxation. Most successful people work smart, but not all of them work hard.

The puritan work ethic may prevent you from faulting this worktape. Many Baby Boomers, especially, believe that hard work is a sign of an upstanding, righteous person. Our parents taught us that hard work is what won the wars and got us out of the Great Depression. If your parents modeled this worktape for you in your growing-up years, you may have a high need to be in control, achieve perfection, and do what others want you to do. You may also measure your own worth by what others think. All of these characteristics are common among children of workaholics.

Obviously, hard work has its place. But we sometimes overstate its value and ignore other important criteria for success. Be on the watch for this "No Pain, No Gain" philosophy of life.

Worktape #4: If You Really Care, You'll Go Beyond the Call of Duty

"We are here to serve people," this worktape repeats over and over. "You have the opportunity to make a difference. If you are truly compassionate and want to help others, you will stay late and come in early."

Yes, you are working in a service profession, and you should be proud of that. However, be careful about becoming a martyr. Caring and serving others doesn't mean you should have no personal boundaries. If you say no to the requests of others now and then, you are not an uncaring person. You are simply a normal human being who, to remain healthy, needs alone time, family time, "off" time.

Moreover, if you over-dedicate your caring self to work hours, you will have little caring left for your family and for yourself. Working in moderation doesn't mean you don't care—it just means that you care about more things in life than work. Work must be balanced with the rest of your life.

Turn Off the Tapes

These caregiver worktapes often result in work addiction. An important step toward having more balance in your life is to consciously hear the worktapes that are the soundtrack behind your behavior. Can you think of any others that influence your particular work patterns? Open up your head and heart and see if you are being driven by worktapes. All change begins with insight. You might find it helpful to explore your worktapes with your responsibility partner.

Understanding Caregiver Burnout

What happens when companions to the dying and the bereaved repeatedly ignore their own grief needs? Sometimes, influences such as bereavement overload (experiencing overwhelming loss within a short time span or, in this case, being around loss too much), unrealistic expectations about helping all the dying and bereaved people in one's community, or discovering that, at times, one cares more about others than one cares about herself or himself, cause burnout.

Symptoms of burnout often include the following:
- Exhaustion and loss of energy
- Irritability and impatience
- Cynicism and detachment
- Physical complaints and depression
- Disorientation and confusion
- Feelings of omnipotence and indispensability
- Minimization and denial of feelings

Let's examine each of these stress-related symptoms and then explore ways in which we as caregivers can strive to companion ourselves in the face of these symptoms.

Exhaustion and loss of energy
Feelings of exhaustion and loss of energy are usually among the first signals of caregiver distress. For many of us, low energy and fatigue can be difficult to acknowledge because they are the opposite of the high energy level required to meet caregiving demands.

Our bodies are powerful instruments and frequently wiser than our minds. Exhaustion and lack of physical and psychic energy are often unconscious "cries for self-help." If we could only slow down and listen to the voice within.

Irritability and impatience

Irritability and impatience are inherent to the experience of caregiver burnout. As effective helpers we typically feel a sense of accomplishment and reward for our efforts. As stress increases, however, our ability to feel reward diminishes while our irritability and impatience become heightened.

Disagreements and a tendency to blame others for interpersonal difficulties may occur as stress takes its toll on our emotional and physical well-being. A telltale sign to watch for: You have more compassion and sensitivity for those you care for at work than you have for your own family.

Cynicism and detachment

As caregivers experiencing emotional fatigue, we may begin to respond to stress in a manner that saves something of ourselves. We may begin to question the value of helping others, of our family life, of friendships, even of life itself. We may work to convince ourselves that "there's no point in getting involved" as we rationalize our need to distance ourselves from the stress of interpersonal encounters.

These feelings of detachment help us distance ourselves from feelings of pain, helplessness, and hurt. I have also observed that a general sense of impatience with those we care for often goes hand-in-hand with cynicism and detachment.

Physical complaints and depression

Physical complaints, real or imagined, are often experienced by caregivers suffering from burnout. Sometimes, physical complaints are easier for us to talk about than emotional concerns. The process of consciously or unconsciously converting emotional conflicts into physical symptoms may result in a variety of bodily problems, such as headaches, stomachaches, backaches, and long-lasting colds.

Generalized feelings of depression are also common to the phenomenon of burnout. Loss of appetite, difficulty sleeping, sudden changes in mood, and lethargy suggest that depression has become a part of the overall stress syndrome. Depression is a constellation of symptoms that together tell us something is wrong and we must pay attention.

Disorientation and confusion

Feelings of disorientation and confusion are often experienced as a component of this syndrome. Our minds may shift from one topic to another, and focusing on current tasks often becomes difficult. We may experience polyphasic behavior, which means we feel busy yet don't accomplish much at all.

Since difficulty focusing results in a lack of a personal sense of competence, confusion only results in more heightened feelings of disorientation. A cycle of confusion resulting in disorientation can develop and become difficult to break. The ability to think clearly suffers; concentration and memory are impaired. In addition, the availability to make decisions and sound judgments becomes limited. If you are

✳✳✳✳✳✳✳✳✳✳✳✳✳✳✳✳✳✳✳✳✳✳✳✳✳✳✳✳

Am I Experiencing Burnout?

A bereavement coordinator for a hospice recently asked me, "How is burnout different from stress?" We might overhear a volunteer or staff person comment, "I'm really feeling burned out today."

Psychologist Christina Maslach, a leading authority on burnout, has outlined three major hallmarks of burnout:

- Emotional exhaustion—feeling drained, not having anything to give even before the day begins
- Depersonalization—feeling disconnected from other people, feeling resentful and seeing them negatively
- Reduced sense of personal accomplishment—feeling ineffective, that the results achieved are not meaningful

Of course, all of us have occasional days when our motivation and energy levels are low. While this fluctuation in energy levels is normal, burnout is an end stage that typically develops over time. Once a person is truly fatigued, dramatic changes are necessary to reverse the process.

Step back for a moment and complete this brief burnout survey. Review your life over the past 12 months and answer the questions with a yes or no:

1. Do you generally feel fatigued and lacking in energy?
2. Are you getting irritable, impatient, and angry with people around you (home and/or work)?
3. Do you feel cynical and detached from the people you companion?
4. Do you suffer from more than your share of physical complaints, such as headaches, stomachaches, backaches, and long-lasting colds?
5. Do you generally feel depressed or notice sudden fluctuations in your moods?
6. Do you feel busy yet sense that you aren't accomplishing much?
7. Do you have difficulty concentrating or remembering?
8. Do you think you have to be the one to help all those people who are dying or experiencing grief?
9. Do you feel less of a sense of satisfaction about your helping efforts than you have in the past?
10. Do you feel that you have nothing left to give?

In general, if you answered yes to 2-4 of the questions, you may be in the early phases of burnout. If you answered yes to 5-7 of these questions, you are quickly moving in the direction of total fatigue. If you answered yes to 8-10 of these questions, you are burned out! If you had 12, get help right now, as there are only 10 questions.

✳✳✳✳✳✳✳✳✳✳✳✳✳✳✳✳✳✳✳✳✳✳✳✳✳✳✳✳

feeling disoriented and confused, your system is overloaded and in need of a break from the continuing cycle of stress.

Omnipotence and indispensability

Another common symptom of burnout is a sense of omnipotence and indispensability. Statements like "No one else can provide the kind of care I can" and "I have to be the one to help these people" are not simply the expressions of a healthy ego.

Other people besides you *can* companion the dying and the bereaved, and many do it very well. When we as caregivers begin to feel indispensable, we tend to block not only our own growth but the growth and healing of others as well.

Minimization and denial of feelings

When stressed to their limits, some caregivers continue to minimize, if not out-and-out deny, feelings of fatigue. The grief and death companion who minimizes is aware of feeling stressed but works to minimize these feelings by diluting them through a variety of rationalizations. From a self-perspective, minimizing stress seems to work, particularly because it is commensurate with the self-imposed principle of "being all things to all people." However, internally repressed feelings of stress build within and emotional strain results.

Perhaps the most dangerous characteristic of burnout is the total denial of feelings of stress. As denial takes over, the caregiver's symptoms of stress become enemies to be fought instead of friends to be understood. Regardless of how loud the mind and body cry out for relief, no one is listening.

"When I began my journey companioning grieving children and families, I was newly married, without children, younger, and more naive. As the years passed and I gained more education and experience, my family grew along with my obligations. The day came when my mentors and supervisor asked me how I took care of myself. I was quick to answer, 'I listen to music, take time for myself, and exercise.' But I wasn't really doing these things with any real intention. Unfortunately, my negligence caught up with me, and I began to experience compassion fatigue and vicarious trauma.

"With a heavy heart, I discussed the possibility of leaving the grief world because of the overwhelming feelings I was experiencing. This was potentially the most valuable step in my self-care process and in my career. In this difficult time, I realized that taking care of yourself is of paramount importance when you have the passion and ability to companion people through their grief.

"I began to look at my self-care in a new way. It wasn't just about listening to music, taking time for myself, or exercising. It was about making an intention and telling myself, 'This is a moment you are taking for yourself.' I continue to listen to music, but instead of simply turning on the radio, I now have a playlist of self-care songs. Instead of just going for a run or playing a game of tennis, I label the activity as follows: 'this exercise today is a way for me to take care of myself.' Alone time now takes the form of meditation, which is how I center and ground myself.

"Labeling self-care may seem like a trivial piece of the self-care process, but for me it made all the difference. It has enabled me to separate, process, and be with my clients in a new way. When I am with them, I am fully present, and when I am without them, I experience full separation."

— Amanda D. Mahoney

The Spillover Effects of Burnout

So far we've been talking about the diminishing and harmful effects of caregiver burnout on the caregiver himself or herself. But because no human being is an island, the effects can extend to everyone who has a relationship with the caregiver.

At work, colleagues are affected. The burned-out caregiver's moods and attitude can permeate the workplace, lowering the morale and effectiveness of everyone around him. How many of us have worked alongside a burned-out caregiver and not been negatively affected by it?

And at home, relationships with significant others, children, and extended family suffer as well. Some people experiencing burnout at work put more pressure on their home and friend relationships in an effort to get their needs for support and understanding met. Others react to burnout by withdrawing from friends and family. Still others transfer their painful thoughts and feelings onto their partners or family members. Consciously or unconsciously, they misattribute their feelings of anger, disappointment, sorrow, and despair to those they're closest to.

Most of us profess that our families are the most important things in our lives, yet honestly, how much of our "best selves" do we devote to family? Finding a healthy work-life balance is challenging for anyone, but for the burned-out caregiver it can seem impossible. After all, you aren't a different person once you get home. Some people think they can compartmentalize their lives in this way…keeping work at work and holding family time separate and sacred.

Yet the reality is that your thoughts and your moods and your feelings and your very soul can't be separated into convenient chunks. You are a whole person, and in many ways you cannot help but bring your whole self to everything you do. Your soul demands congruency, and when you are living incongruently, your soul lets you know it is suffering.

So yes, burnout can and does spill over into all facets of our lives. I have seen it destroy marriages, ruin friendships, and mar children's growing-up years. The good news is that it's never too late to acknowledge burnout and take actions to rebalance your life.

Emotional Involvement and Stress

The reasons caregivers to the dying and bereaved feel stress are often many and complex. When we care deeply for people in grief, we open ourselves to our own vulnerabilities related to loss issues. Perhaps another person's grief stimulates memories of old griefs of our own. Perhaps those we wish to help actually frustrate our efforts to be supportive.

Whatever the reason, the natural way to prevent ourselves from being hurt or disappointed is to deny feelings in general. Ironically, the denial of feelings is often accompanied by an internal sense of a lack of purpose. This is because the willingness and ability to feel are ultimately what give meaning to life.

Of all the stresses death and grief companions are subject to, emotional involvement is central to the potential for burnout. Perhaps we should ask ourselves what we lose when we decide to minimize or ignore the significant level of emotional involvement intrinsic to caring for the dying and the bereaved. We probably will discover that in the process of minimizing or ignoring, we are, in fact, eliminating our potential to help people move toward a sense of inner peace. As the saying goes, "If you want to help others, the place to start is with yourself."

We probably need to remind ourselves that we are our own most important helping instrument and that what we know about ourselves makes a tremendous difference in our capacity to assist others. While the admirable goal of helping grieving and dying people may alone seem to justify emotional sacrifices, ultimately we are not helping others effectively when we ignore what we are experiencing within ourselves.

Obviously, we cannot draw close to others without beginning to affect and be affected by them. This is the nature of the helping relationship with those confronting death. We cannot help others from a protective position. Helping occurs openly when we are defenseless—if we allow ourselves to be. My experience suggests that it takes practice to work toward an understanding of what is taking place inside oneself while at the same time trying to grasp what is taking place inside others. After all, these related thoughts and feelings occur simultaneously and are significantly interrelated.

Involving yourself with others, particularly at a time of death and grief, requires taking care of yourself as well as others. Emotional overload, circumstances surrounding death, and caring about the bereaved will unavoidably result in times of caregiver fatigue. When this occurs, we should feel no sense of inadequacy or stigma if we, too, need the support and understanding of a counselor. As a matter of fact, we should be proud of ourselves if we care enough about "caring for the caregiver" that we seek out just such a relationship! Even if you don't feel a need for a counseling relationship for yourself, I strongly suggest that all death and grief companions have a "responsibility partner" with whom to debrief and exchange mutual support.

The Overcaring Caregiver

Do you care too much about those you companion? Do you care more about helping them than they do themselves? Do you feel it is your duty to worry about all dying and bereaved people and get involved with their problems? On the other hand, do you feel "used" by some bereaved families?

If you've answered yes to some or all of these questions, you may be at risk for being an overcaring caregiver.

But what is an overcaring caregiver? I define it this way: someone who continually puts the needs of the dying and the bereaved before her own, ultimately to the caregiver's detriment. The overcaring caregiver appears to feed on providing support and comfort to others; however, self-care needs are often minimized, denied, or completely over-looked. She, in fact, does help those in her care, but she usually wonders if she helped enough or "did it right."

The overcaring caregiver often confuses caregiving with caretaking. Caretakers—those with a desire to "rescue"—often become overattached to the people they companion, becoming responsible *for* them instead of *to* them.

When we focus all of our energy on people and problems outside of ourselves, little time is left for self-understanding. As a consequence, one of the primary symptoms of the overcaring caregiver is a lack of awareness of the dynamics of caring too much. This lack of awareness may result in feelings of helplessness and frustration, which are in turn are sometimes expressed in the form of obsessing and worrying about one's clients.

Now a vicious cycle is set in motion. The more the helper ruminates about the client's problems (obviously, worrying doesn't really change anything), the higher the need becomes to rescue. Therefore, more inappropriate over-involvement occurs, with the focus staying outside of oneself.

Why Caregivers Care Too Much

- *Unreconciled personal grief.* As my research on this phenomenon has progressed, it has become increasingly obvious that some people enter into death and grief caregiving as a conscious or unconscious attempt to heal their own grief. The desire to "fix" someone else's grief is often a projection of a need to "fix" one's own grief. When this occurs, it is a classic form of displacement. The displacer is the person who takes the expression of grief away from personal loss and displaces the feelings in other directions. In this situation, the focus is on the caretaking (rescuing) of other people.

- *Family of origin issues.* I have found that many caregivers to the dying and the bereaved were helpers in their families of origin. They may have assumed the responsibility of resolving family conflicts or disciplining other children. In adulthood, they are often those who sponsor family reunions or organize holiday gatherings.

- *Socially learned personality characteristics.* Many caregivers are particularly sensitive to the needs of others. Sometimes this sensitivity goes beyond empathy to over-identification with the suffering of others. It's almost as if they feel most comfortable when they are with people in emotional pain.

Consequences of Caring Too Much

There are a wide variety of fallout consequences when care-givers care too much:

- A broad constellation of stress-related symptoms, such as exhaustion and loss of energy, irritability and impatience, cynicism and detachment, physical illness (real or imagined), omnipotence and feeling indispensable, minimization and denial of feelings.

- Deterioration in relationships with family and friends.

- Symptoms of depression, sleeping difficulties, and low self-esteem.

- A displacement of compulsive behavior into other areas of life, such as spending money, overachievement, or drug and alcohol abuse.

✳✳✳✳✳✳✳✳✳✳✳✳✳✳✳✳✳✳✳✳

Signs and Symptoms That You Care Too Much

- A tendency to try to please others instead of yourself
- A need for approval and a tendency to feel safest when giving
- A desire to "solve" people's problems rather than create conditions that allow you to move toward reconciliation of your own issues
- A tendency to over-extend and over-commit
- A desire to do things for people that they are capable of doing themselves
- A denial of your own need for support and understanding, resulting in the myth of the "super-caregiver" or "being all things to all people"
- A tendency to "feel different" from or "more special" than other people
- A desire to be and act extremely responsible. You may secretly like to be on 24-hour call while trying to give the appearance of resenting it
- A tendency to want to continually "check on" those in your care
- A desire to be "in control" and a belief that you know how to "make things turn out well" for dying and bereaved people
- A tendency to need your clients as much as, if not more than, they need you
- A tendency to neglect your own intimate relationships in favor of helping "needy clients"

✳✳✳✳✳✳✳✳✳✳✳✳✳✳✳✳✳✳✳✳

The Perfectionistic Caregiver

Have you ever noticed the tendency among us caregivers to be rather perfectionistic? This section will help you review whether you suffer from this imbalance and explore some ways of accepting how imperfect we all really are.

Check off the following if they apply to you:

_____ I tend to lose patience with people if they aren't quick learners.

_____ I have a reputation as being someone who is difficult to please.

_____ I tend to want to do things exactly right every time I do something.

_____ I get upset with myself when I don't do something well.

_____ I tend to think I only have one opportunity to do things right, so I better not mess up.

_____ I get frustrated when I play games and don't perform well.

If you answered yes to most of these questions, you may well suffer from perfectionism. At times it's hard to acknowledge this is an issue in your life, so you may want the opinion of friends and family who observe you.

Let's look at a formal definition:

Perfectionism: to be perfect, having a reputation of always being right and reliable, exceptional.

✳✳✳✳✳✳✳✳✳✳✳✳✳✳✳✳✳✳✳✳✳✳✳✳

Counseling for the Caregiver

The wise caregiver will find other caregivers with whom to
explore the ways in which companioning the dying and the
bereaved impacts one's life. Unreflective work with those in pain
can lead to failure in self-companionship and can contribute to
the ever-hovering symptoms of caregiver fatigue and depression. Moreover, lack of personal introspection may result in
grandiose rescue fantasies and lack of attention to self-needs.
Unfortunately, because we as caregivers are often taught to
appear knowledgeable and "in control," self-companionship
can be more difficult for us than for many others.

The empathetic attachment to people in pain naturally results in
awareness of any pain in the caregiver's own life. Added to this
is the reality that sometimes our interest in helping others grows
from unresolved pains in our own childhoods. Obviously, good
self-companionship in part involves staying conscious of our
helping motives and how the caregiving experience influences
the embracing of our own life hurts, old or new.

So, do I recommend counseling for the caregiver? Absolutely.
Personal counseling is nothing to be ashamed of; indeed, it
should be thought of as part of our ongoing desire to stay in
touch with ourselves and others. Supervision and regular
debriefing is not only wise, it is invaluable to managing the
ongoing demands that come with death and grief companioning. We understand the importance of regular medical check-
ups. Shouldn't we also go in for an occasional emotional and
spiritual check-up? At minimum, be sure you have selected and
make frequent use of your responsibility partner.

✳✳✳✳✳✳✳✳✳✳✳✳✳✳✳✳✳✳✳✳✳✳✳✳

Why are some caregivers driven by perfectionism? Often it's related to control. Perfectionists tend to feel safer, more in charge.

The problem: You risk having your identity merged with perfectionism. While, at bottom, you realize you are not perfect, it's difficult to admit you aren't. You may find yourself working harder to maintain this image by saying yes when you mean no or by being more available to others while becoming unavailable to your family and friends.

You may find yourself placing high standards on yourself even when you are supposed to be playing a game and having fun. The result is that not only do you not have fun, the people you "play" with don't enjoy your company anymore.

Perfectionism creates an energy drain and puts you at high risk for burnout. Your need to be in control has the potential of spiraling out of control.

Self-companionship Cures for Perfectionism

Strive for imperfection. What? That's hard to do when you have been trying to be perfect for so long. What I mean is to free yourself to not be perfect. Take the pressure off—play a game but allow yourself to relax, laugh, and plan to lose.

Allow yourself to make mistakes. An occasional mistake makes you human.

Remind yourself of your successes, not your mistakes.

Look for creative ways to free yourself from compulsive perfectionism. In the end you will gain more energy, joy, and time to relax and simply be!

So, do you feel you understand my philosophy of companioning the dying and the bereaved, and have you given thought to your own caregiving philosophy? Are you convinced that good self-companionship is essential? Have you explored your own personal loss history and caregiving motivations? Have you acknowledged that your life may be out of balance and that you need to focus more on self-care? Have you explored potential symptoms of burnout and perfectionism in yourself?

If you've answered "yes" to these questions, you're ready to embark on a self-companioning makeover. The steps set forth in Part Two of this book can help you not only rebalance your life but transform your very existence. You can proceed knowing that you are never alone. You can tap into this grace whenever you need it, giving you a courage you may not have known you had before. Are you ready?

✳✳✳✳✳✳✳✳✳✳✳✳✳✳✳✳✳✳✳✳✳✳✳✳✳✳✳✳✳

Organizational Stress

In caregiving professions, we usually choose our careers for altruistic reasons, but we sometimes find ourselves spending much of our time filling out forms to keep up with mandated regulations or complying with the demands of supervisors who seem more concerned about how many visits we had with patients and families than with the quality of the visits. Also, as organizations get bigger, I have observed two all-too-common causes of burnout:

1. Role overload

    While it doesn't happen in all hospices, I have seen cases in which a staff member is required to serve in multiple roles. For example, if a staff member is expected to be the bereavement coordinator *and* director of volunteers as well as write the quarterly newsletter, keep up the website, etc., what do you think will happen? Being spread too thin puts her at huge risk for burning out on the job. She may try to fulfill all the obligations for a while, but she will eventually, through no fault of her own, break down...and then the organization will simply replace her and expect the new person to take on all the same roles. The cycle just repeats itself.

2. Lack of rewards

    As organizations grow, they sometimes forget about the critical importance of appreciation, recognition, and rewards. This can put the staff members at risk for discouragement and eventually burnout. A basic research finding is that employees are more able to cope with stress and the demands of a job when they feel appreciated and adequately rewarded. When this does not happen, individual and organizational burnout can set in.

    Sadly, organizational departments that do human caregiving but don't have a strictly medical focus are often referred to as the "soft" areas of the organization, as if they are somehow less valuable than the "real" care. In other words, because a hospice still operates within a medical model, there is a hierarchy about the "most important areas of caregiving." When and if budgets are cut, the "soft" caregivers are the people who are more likely to be let go. Some organizations only have certain staff positions because they are mandated to do so, but if there is a lack of support and understanding of the value of these positions, people know it, feel it, and experience it, resulting in demoralization and burnout. If soul-based care isn't valued where you work, stay aware of this and try to take care of yourself through excellent self-companionship.

✳✳✳✳✳✳✳✳✳✳✳✳✳✳✳✳✳✳✳✳✳✳✳✳✳✳✳✳✳

Part Two

An Eight-Week
Self-Companioning Makeover
for Caregivers to the Dying
and the Bereaved

Before You Begin

Perhaps we should remember that just as healing in grief is a process, so too is recovering from the normal challenges of this area of caregiving as well as from overcaring and perfectionism in our work with dying and bereaved people. Don't blame or shame yourself if you recognize some parts of yourself herein. Be compassionate with yourself as you acknowledge any potential problems, and be hopeful that you can make some positive changes.

If as you worked through Part 1 of this book you recognized symptoms of unreconciled personal grief, burnout, overcaring, or perfectionism in yourself, this makeover is for you. I've intentionally chosen the term "makeover" because, as any reality TV fan can tell you, makeovers are fun and exciting. Even though they can be a little unpredictable and emotionally challenging, makeovers almost always achieve positive, transforming results.

So I invite you to engage in this self-companioning makeover in the same spirit. Think of it as something fun and exciting—something that has the potential to transform your life for the better.

When I teach the art of companioning the dying and the bereaved, I often talk about the concept of "perturbation." As you know, when people actively grieve and mourn, there is movement. In other words, their emotions are in motion. The term "perturbation" refers to the capacity to experience change and movement. To integrate grief, people must be touched by what they experience. When they cannot feel a feeling, on the other hand, they are unable to be changed by it, and instead of experiencing perturbation, they become "stuck."

Do you feel similarly stuck in your habits of overcaring for the dying and the bereaved? Are you ignoring or repressing your own needs? If so, it's time to create some "perturbation" in your routine—and in your heart and soul! This makeover will do just that.

I've structured the makeover as an eight-week process. Each week you will bite off one major task before progressing to the following week's challenge. This does not mean, of course, that you will "finish" each task in one week. Like grief, this makeover is not an event; instead, it is an ongoing process. In fact, the last week's task is called Revise, which means go back to the first week and start over.

Still, each time you work the eight-week process, you will be making progress. And even if you actively work through it just once, it can't help but begin to stir your psychic pot— creating perturbation that will begin to effect change, whether you are aware of it or not.

I strongly recommend working through the makeover process with someone else, preferably a colleague or work peer such as your responsibility partner. First of all, pairing up with someone else will make both of you more accountable for finishing the process. And secondly, while fun and exciting, this process may also spark painful personal revelations—the kind that need to be voiced aloud to someone with a compassionate, nonjudgmental listening ear.

You and your responsibility partner should meet at least once a week during the eight-week period. At your first meeting, which should take place before you begin the makeover, I recommend discussing the content in Part 1 of this book. Talk about each of the concepts and how they apply to your partner and to you. Discuss the self-assessments and what they may have revealed about your own situations. Then schedule a regular meeting time to share your unique experiences each week as you follow the makeover process.

I also recommend keeping a caregivers' journal as you step through the makeover. The journal will be the place where you can "put" all your thoughts and feelings related to the change process. It will be the place where you can answer the questions asked each week. And it will be the record of your journey, so that the next time you choose to engage with the eight-week process, you can see where the perturbation took you and celebrate how far you've already come.

As with any self-help program, this one will require your commitment, time, and attention to be effective. And if you're like most of the nurturing caregivers I know, you're not naturally very good at focusing your commitment, time, and attention on yourself (although you're probably *exceedingly* good at lavishing those resources on everyone else!). But remember this: Any time you spend on your self-companioning makeover will actually make you a better caregiver. So it's a win-win-win situation—for you, for your friends and family, *and* for your clients.

Week 1: Acknowledge the Reality of Any Imbalances and Surrender to Them

I often talk about the six needs that all mourners must meet if they are to heal and grow through their grief. The first need is to acknowledge the reality of the death. Similarly, *your* first need in reconstructing your work life is to acknowledge any imbalances you may have uncovered in Part 1 of this book and surrender to them.

As caregivers, our tendency is to say, "I'm fine! How are *you?*" But this week, your challenge is to say, to yourself and to your responsibility partner, "You know what? I'm not fine. What are my self-care challenges?" If you are in the habit of putting on a false mask of cheer around your coworkers, friends, and family, this is also the week for you to start being more honest with them.

When you adopt a policy of honesty, you stop trying to hold back the flood you may have been holding back for a long time. You stop resisting and instead, you surrender to your situation exactly as it is. When you do this, things begin to change. *Surrender* is, in part, about accepting the reality that you even though you have tried, you have been unable to control circumstances and make everything right. Your resistance has been an instinctive defense mechanism, which you used to push away or deny your pain.

When you surrender to your situation exactly as it is, you acknowledge, "This is what I'm faced with right now in my life's journey. While I'd like it to be different, I must allow myself to face the reality of what is happening." When you surrender, you release attachment to how you feel your life should be and invite yourself to be in the presence of your life exactly as it is.

Surrender is an act of courage that allows you to detach from the outcome. In surrender, you become more capable of seeing choices that were concealed from you. In surrender, you are invited to stop trying to control what you cannot control. The gifts of peace of mind and gentleness of heart await you. By allowing yourself to surrender to the truth of your situation, you create conditions for something new to arise from within yourself—out of the dark and into the light!

Next week you'll spend more time naming exactly what's out of balance, what's not "fine." For now, all you have to do is admit to yourself and to anyone else you choose that you are aware all is not well.

Questions to answer in your journal then discuss with your partner:

1. How are you feeling about your work-life balance right now and why?

2. Rate your satisfaction with your work-life balance on a scale of 1 to 10, with 1 being extremely dissatisfied and 10 being extremely satisfied.

3. In your career as a caregiver to the dying and the bereaved, how has your work-life balance changed over the years? Draw a graph that visually shows this.

4. Draw an old-fashioned teeter-totter. Write "work" on the left plank and "personal" on the right plank. Now, on top of each plank, write down the tasks and people that are consuming most of your time and energy right now. After you've finished writing, ask yourself which direction the teeter-totter would tip if it was real.

5. Write about the concept of surrender and how you feel about accepting your life exactly as it is right now. Note that this doesn't mean you don't want your life to change; it just means you are nonjudgmentally looking at your life and saying, "Yes. I see you."

A few ideas to help you embrace this week's challenge:

- *Love yourself.*

  For caregivers, it is usually easier to express love to others than it is ourselves. Yet, by feeling your own love in a more direct way, you can be transformed and open yourself to new spiritual understandings. Loving yourself starts with accepting yourself. If you, as a living, unique human being, are unable to value who you are, who can? Loving yourself means recognizing you, seeing you, and honoring you. In part, it is about celebrating yourself. It is a privilege to be you. You have been given the opportunity to feel, to see, to live life with both its challenges and opportunities. Sometimes, in the midst of the challenges of life, you can forget this. Yet always remember: It is a gift to be alive, and just being born into the world is a privilege.

- *Sigh.*

  Sighing is an expression of letting go. When we sigh, we resign ourselves to something. We accept something, though perhaps it is something we didn't want to accept. In Romans 8 it says that when there are no words for our prayer, the spirits intervene and pray for us in sighs deeper than anything that can be expressed in words. Sigh deeply. Sigh whenever you feel like it. With each sigh, you are acknowledging that you are not in total control of your life. You are accepting what is. Each sigh is your prayer.

- *Just be.*

  You may have heard it said that there is no past, there is no future, there is only this moment. In *The Power of Now*, Eckhart Tollé encourages us to truly be present in the current moment. "Life is now," he writes. "There was never a time when your life was not now, nor will there ever be... Nothing ever happened in the past; it happened in the Now. Nothing will ever happen in the future; it will happen in the Now." The challenge is that it is really hard to live in the moment. Our minds constantly revisit the past and think forward to the future. Our egos dwell on what was and what will be. Tollé and others believe that your mind is different from your spirit. Your mind is the house of the ego; your soul is the house of the spirit. Your spirit—your essence—can observe the egoic antics of the mind. Your ego is earthbound; your spirit is timeless. The next time your mind takes you away from the present and into worry and fear, allow your spirit to watch your mind and smile at its earthly obsessions.

Week 2: Inventory Any Hurts and Unhappiness You Are Experiencing

For the past week, you've done the hard work of acknowledging that there's an imbalance and surrendering to the reality of your life exactly as it is. From the bottom of my heart, congratulations. For many caregivers I know, Week 1 proves the most difficult challenge of all.

This week I want you to start teasing apart exactly what isn't working. Sometimes when we are depressed or fatigued, we have a hard time identifying what's wrong. We're just "sad" or "tired." But to start making improvements in your work life, you'll have to begin paying attention to what bothers you *in particular*.

As you move through the coming week, keep a pad of paper or your makeover journal handy to jot down notes. Whenever you feel a wave or a blip of sadness, frustration, guilt, anger, anxiety, or other painful emotion, make a note about what you were doing, what you were feeling, and why.

Caregivers often have a hard time acknowledging "negative" emotions in themselves (although as you know and probably counsel those in your care, no feeling is truly negative—it simply is), so you may need to consciously practice heightening your self-awareness of such thoughts and feelings and, again, acknowledging that they even exist.

If that's true for you, start paying attention to your "gut reactions"—those visceral twinges in your solar plexus that are your intuitive and perhaps most true and unfiltered responses. If your gut is saying "no" even though your logical mind and your selfless work ethic are saying "yes," take heed and write it down.

Of course, your work life is not distinct and inseparable from your personal life. This is especially true for caregivers to the dying and the bereaved, who tend to care very deeply for their clients. And on the flip side, your personal life is inextricable from your work life because you bring the whole of who you are to both your caregiving and your personal relationships. So take notes at home as well as at work.

This is also the week to look more closely at your personal loss history, any current losses you may be experiencing, and your motivations for becoming (and remaining) a caregiver to the dying and the bereaved.

By the end of the week, you may have quite an inventory of hurts and unhappiness in your life. In your weekly meeting with your responsibility partner, discuss what you found and also highlight the three most painful realities you wrote down. They might be relatively insignificant things ("I feel resentful that I never get to take a lunch break") or colossal quandaries ("I feel such despair whenever I walk through the front door"). No matter how big or little, they should be the three issues that hit your gut—and your heart—the hardest.

The process of enumerating your dissatisfactions takes them out of the realm of the mythic and into the realm of the seeable, touchable, and, thus, changeable. If you can explain it, you can share it with yourself and with others. And if you can do that, you can figure out how to either change it or, if it's outside your control, change your response to it.

Questions to answer in your journal then discuss with your partner:

1. If you haven't already, write down the answers to the personal loss background, current issues, and motivations questions on pages 25 through 33.

2. Make a two-column list. In the left column, write down all the things you love about your work and your life. In the right column, write down all the things in your work and your life that make you feel stressed, anxious, unhappy, irritated, numb, or angry.

3. Now draw a big empty cloud. Inside the cloud, write a word for each thing you feel is missing in your life. These words could describe general concepts (such as "balance" or "a close relationship with my husband") or more specific deficits (such as "cardiovascular exercise" or "an annual 2-week vacation") or, most likely, a mixture of both.

4. What are the three most gut-level painful things in the right column of your two-column list and the three in your deficit cloud? Highlight all six of them with a bright-colored highlighter, then rewrite them, one per page, at the top of a fresh, blank journal page. For each of these new "challenge pages," fill the page by writing about why you think this situation has arisen. What is the root cause of the problem? When you've finished writing about all six problems, ask yourself if you can see any common root causes among the six.

A few ideas to help you embrace this week's challenge:

- *Cry.*

  As you know, tears are a natural cleansing and healing mechanism. They rid your body of stress chemicals. If as you work through this makeover process you feel like crying, cry. (On the other hand, don't feel bad if you aren't crying a lot. Not everyone is a crier.) Examining your losses and your disappointments and your weaknesses is challenging, difficult work that will naturally bring up feelings of grief. And you of all people should know that it's important to express your grief! So go ahead and cry or do whatever you need to do to express your thoughts and feelings as you progress through the coming weeks.

- *Allow yourself to receive.*

  Most of us caregivers are better at giving than receiving. Yet, there is a reciprocal relationship between the two. In order to receive, we must give. And in order to give, we must receive. Ask your responsibility partner or another supportive friend to assist you with the following. Sit across from each other. Be silent for two to three minutes, then have your friend tell you something they admire or appreciate about you. Be receptive. Take in what your friend shares with an open heart. Notice where you are uncomfortable or find yourself wanting to discount what your friend says. Breathe deeply for a minute as you continue to open yourself to this gift of receiving. Sit with it until you can fully accept this verbal gift. Show your gratitude by nonverbally saying thank you. Carry out the same process outlined above for your friend. Then repeat the process, going to a deeper level of truth. Observe how your connection and bond with your friend increases. As you learn to receive and give, the separation between giver and receiver disappears.

- *Believe in your capacity to thrive.*
  Many caregivers before you have struggled with the same self-companionship challenges you are struggling with. And those who have chosen to be active participants in their own lives would want me to tell you this: Within you is the capacity to live the life of your dreams. While you cannot totally control your life, you can rebalance it. And you can choose to respond to external events in ways that will bring you joy and peace.

"As one who cares for the dying and the bereaved, follow God's command to 'clothe yourself with compassion, kindness, humility, gentleness, and patience' (Colossians 3:12). I have found this the key in my ministry of over 25 years. Engage in a hobby as well as do things socially. Remember that what you are is a gift from God, but what you make of yourself is a gift to God!"

— Reba David

Week 3: Create a Vision for Moving Forward and Set Your Intention

So far you've acknowledged your work/life imbalance, looked it in the face, and begun to identify its root causes. (Note: I realize that uncovering root causes is a challenging task that takes many people years of exploration to really achieve. For purposes of this eight-week makeover, simply beginning the process of trying to reveal and articulate root causes is enough to create some perturbation and nudge you in the right direction.) This week you'll be spending some time envisioning your life the way you *want* it to be instead.

Hopes and dreams are indeed powerful things, but what I've learned over the years is that if they're never acknowledged, put to paper, and shared with others, they have a tragic way of never being fulfilled. You see, it's easy and it feels good to dream within the safety of our own minds. But when we voice our dreams out loud, they become goals that we risk never reaching. Putting ourselves out there in that way is scary. Yet it is the very act of taking this risk that has the potential to move you from where you are to where you want to be.

"All our dreams can come true…," famously said that greatest of dreamers, Walt Disney, "if we have the courage to pursue them." So yes, this week you must take all the hopes and dreams you have inside you and express them outside yourself.

First, spend some time writing out your answers to the questions at the end of this section. Whether your vision is fuzzy or crystal-clear to you, it's still helpful to write it down.

I also invite you to create a vision board, which is a collage of words and images that capture the life you envision. Sit down with a stack of magazines or browse online and look for photos, illustrations, and headlines that depict your hopes and dreams. Cut them out, then arrange and paste them onto a piece of poster board. Then place your poster board somewhere you will see it often and be able to linger on it.

Once you've crafted your vision as well as you can, you must next set your intention to achieve it. Intention is defined as being conscious of what you want to experience. A close cousin of "affirmation," it is using the power of positive thought to produce a desired result. With commitment and intention you can and will move in the direction of your dreams.

This concept of intention-setting presupposes that your outer reality is a direct reflection of your inner thoughts and feelings. If you can mold some of your beliefs, you can influence your reality. Your beliefs have the power to help you rebalance your life. If you routinely remind yourself that you can and will move in the direction of a more joyful life, you will be setting a course of divine momentum toward your goals.

I always encourage mourners to become "active participants" instead of "passive witnesses" in their grief journeys. I tell them that they can achieve healing and transformation through active engagement with and expression of their thoughts and feelings. Likewise, you hold within you the power to heal your work-life imbalance, but only if you actively participate.

Action, then, picks up where intention-setting leaves off. If you are actively stepping through this eight-week makeover, especially if you are doing it "out loud," together with a responsibility partner, you are already taking action. And you'll soon be taking more. Weeks four through seven in this program are all about taking more action.

Set your intention to rebalance your life, then, slowly and in doses, take actions that move you in the direction of your vision. Set your intention to self-companion, then take actions to nurture yourself. You get the idea. Intention plus action equals a life lived deeply and on purpose.

Questions to answer in your journal then discuss with your partner:

1. What does your well-balanced life look like? What does it feel like?

2. What are you doing during your working hours in this life? Where are you working? How are you interacting with clients and colleagues?

3. Create a vision board as described in this section.

4. Set your intention to achieve your vision in at least two ways. Writing your intentions in your journal can be one way, but sharing your intentions out loud to at least one other person *in addition to your responsibility partner* who cares and will encourage you is also required.

A few ideas to help you embrace this week's challenge:

- *Live on purpose.*

  Do you believe that things happen for a reason? Do you think that you attract what you are thinking about? I'm not 100 percent sold on the popular concept of the power of attraction, but I have noticed that if I live with awareness and intention, I am able to live my best life. If you set your intention to become an excellent self-companion, and if you move forward each day embracing hope, you are living on purpose. You are living with an awareness that your intentional thoughts create, in part, your destiny. You are a miracle. Your life is a miracle. Live it with the awe and wonder it deserves.

- *Seek your Higher Self.*

  When you "live" in the realm of the Higher Self, you befriend divine qualities that are within you, such as caring, joy, strength, appreciation, and love. The Higher Self is the spiritual part of who you are. While the Higher Self recognizes that challenges and sadness are part of the journey, it also realizes that you can not only survive but go on to thrive. The Higher Self knows that all situations in life—happy and sad—can be used as times to learn and grow. It doesn't see the outside world as a threat; it sees it as a place to contribute and be hopeful about the future. The Higher Self believes that out of the dark comes light, but that you must descend into exploring your hurts and losses before you transcend into experiencing joy.

- *Manifest.*

  Like many caregivers (including, maybe, you!), I believe in callings. I believe that many people, perhaps all people, have feelings deep down inside about why they are here on Earth and what they are meant to do. I feel deeply that my calling is to help others learn to mourn well so they can go on to live well and love well. I know it's my calling because when I'm engaged in my teaching and writing, as I am right now, I feel joyful and in-the-moment. I feel energized and in touch with my center. Many people are afraid to engage with their calling because it seems frivolous or risky. Yet they continue to harbor a longing for it—a wistful longing that leaves them feeling frustrated, stuck, and sad. Now is the time to manifest your true self, to make it a reality. Keep in mind that you don't have to turn your current life upside down. You just have to take one small step today and another small step tomorrow and so on.

"I am a wife, mother, and funeral director for over 25 years. I am not really sure of how I take care of 'me' while doing all of that, but here are some things I do:

- I pray. And I always try to start my day in a positive way by saying I love you, good morning, etc. to others and meaning it.

- I have learned that sleep is very important. I can't help others if I am tired or stressed myself.

- Laughing always helps too. Being positive and speaking words that encourage, even in the darkest hours... People need to see your light.

- I like to surround myself with positive people, too. There really is no time on this earth for negativity.

When I leave my job, I am able to turn off a switch in my brain and find love from my family and friends, who lift me up tremendously! My motto is no problems—only solutions...and God will take care of the rest!"

— Pat Moore

Week 4: Set Aside Time *Each And Every Day From Now On* To Touch Base With Your Spirit

Your spirit is your pure, true self. It is the you that existed before you were born to this temporary earthly existence and the you that will continue on forever after you leave Earth. It is your essence, your soul, your divine spark.

Yet if you're like most people, you pay it little attention. Every day you engage in rituals of self-care. You brush your teeth. You shower. You eat breakfast. Perhaps you read the newspaper or check your e-mail. You say hello to your family or coworkers or neighbors. You take care of your body. You take care of your brain. You probably take care of your social self. But do you take care of your spiritual self each and every day?

If your life is out of balance, it is because you have fallen victim to the myths of modern-day humanity, which champion doing over being and mind and body over spirit. Yet unhappiness, fear, anxiety, and those other challenging emotions we discussed are what you feel when your divine spark has been muted.

It's time to start actively listening to your spirit—not occasionally, but consistently. Because if your spirit is your true self, shouldn't it guide you each and every day? In fact, it's the *not listening* to spirit that was probably the main contributor to your current imbalance. You can connect with your spirit in ways ranging from meditation to prayer, from inspirational reading to listening to or playing music, from walking in the woods to strolling on the beach.

So starting today, I challenge you to set aside 15 minutes (or more) a day to connect with that still, small voice inside you. If you can begin to do that, you will soon see that these 15 minutes are the hub of your day. Your spirit time will center and anchor you, enabling you to proceed through all the other busy hours of your day with a sense of groundedness and peace.

You can spend your 15 spirit-minutes a day doing any number of things. Deep breathing or meditation will not only calm your physical heart but will also help to direct your attention to your innermost feelings. When you are feeling stressed and out of balance, take a deep breath and release whatever is on your mind, allow your body to relax, and experience your connection to the larger whole. Joy and peace are all around you.

Questions to answer in your journal then discuss with your partner:

1. How have you tried to connect with your spirit in the past? Write about all the spiritual practices you have tried and what worked and what didn't.

2. The practice of meditation is thought by many to be the key to connecting with spirit. Have you tried (or are you willing to try) meditation daily? If yes, how did it work for you? If no, what might work for you instead?

3. Write about how you plan to spend your 15 daily spirit-minutes in the coming month.

A few ideas to help you embrace this week's challenge:

- *Meditate.*
  Meditation can change your life. The benefits are physical, emotional, and spiritual. Meditation invites your body into a more relaxed state, promoting more restful sleep, lowering your blood pressure, increasing oxygen circulation and your ability to concentrate, calming your mind, and stimulating an overall feeling of wellbeing. And there are many different kinds of meditation, including some that incorporate movement (such as walking). Start spending 15 minutes a day connecting with your spirit through meditation and I guarantee that in a matter of weeks, your life will begin to be transformed.

- *Pray.*
  Prayer is spirit time because it involves reaching deep within yourself for your most fervent, sacred thoughts and feelings and then articulating them. Even when you pray silently, you're forming words for your thoughts and feelings and you're offering up those words to a presence outside yourself.

- *Listen to music.*
  Music, perhaps more than any other external experience, has the capacity to bring you home to yourself and to put you in touch with your spirit. Beautiful music can communicate to you on many different levels. Music can take you to your favorite place or to another world. Music transforms you, taking you to a "safe place" in your soul, helping you feel that you and the world around you are filled with grace and peace. Music can uplift your mood, soothe you when you are agitated, and open you to harmony, beauty, love, and generosity. Beautiful music that nurtures your being is by its very nature healing. It restores and relaxes you in ways beyond words. Music allows you to access spirit through sound.

- *Create a personal sanctuary just for you.*

  To do the hard work of rebalancing your life, you may need a dedicated safe space to call your own, a private territory where you can explore self-development and spiritual practices as well as read good books, meditate, journal, or simply contemplate the universe. When you understand that contemplate means "to create a space for the divine to enter," perhaps you can acknowledge how important that space can be to your well-being. Find a cozy chair and consider installing a tabletop fountain. You may want to be able to play gentle music or other soothing sounds like ocean waves, birdsong, or gentle drops of the rainforest. Or, maybe you want this space to be dedicated to silence. As Thomas Moore wisely noted, "Silence allows many sounds to reach awareness that otherwise would be unheard."

"A number of years ago I took a palliative care volunteer course at our local hospital. Little did I know how useful this would be when my 76-year-old, very fit husband was unexpectedly diagnosed with Stage IV cancer. Having chosen to home nurse him and love him to death, I knew I had to set up ways that took care of me when he became housebound.

"So I e-mailed a group of friends asking if they would be prepared to form a palliative care team when the time came and come in once a week for a couple of hours to relieve me. To our astonishment, 35 people said yes.

"From the first week of September 2010 to the last week of October, they came. Every day I had a break. Some days I had coffee with a friend or went and sat by the river and cried. Some days I walked briskly until I was out of breath. I went for a pedicure, attended art exhibits or afternoon concerts, spent time nurturing my garden. Whenever possible I found things to laugh at, to marvel about. I got a new hairstyle, bought a new dress. I was never away for more than a couple of hours, usually while Stuart was sleeping.

"I have never done anything as hard or as rewarding or as spiritually uplifting. After his death it was a great comfort to me to know I had loved and cared for him till death do us part in a way that no one else could have."

— Jill Summerhayes

Week 5: Rebalance Your Daily Habits And Schedule

How is your daily spirit-time practice going? I hate to be a stickler, but if you're not faithfully spending at least 15 minutes a day connecting with your spirit, I want you to pause this eight-week makeover and keep working on Week 4 until you make it a habit. It's that essential. The makeover has little transformative power without it.

If you're ready for Week 5, grab your calendar, your journal, and a pencil. It's time to take a very concrete look at how you spend your time.

Time is our currency here on Earth. Many work-life imbalances stem from time-allotment troubles, but it's hard to discern that unless you take a cold, hard, honest look at how you spend your time.

Answer the questions and do the activities suggested at the end of this section. When you compare your actual life to your vision life, are there big discrepancies in how you are spending your time or the amount of time you are spending on certain activities?

Think of your day or your week as a teeter-totter, similar to the one you drew during Week 1. To balance it, you need to actively and purposefully find a mix of habits and activities that meet your needs. If your teeter-totter is steeply tipped toward work, how can you rebalance your schedule?

Of course, shuffling quantities of time alone will not entirely correct any imbalances you may be experiencing because *quality* of time is just as important. But for this week, don't worry about that. Whether you realize it or not, your daily spirit time is hard at work improving the quality of your days, and Weeks 6 and 7 are all about quality as well. So for now, focus on rearranging your daily and weekly calendar in an effort to create a conscious mix of minutes that is in alignment with your vision.

"For years I did not care for myself while caring for others and physically and emotionally paid the price. Once I took my own advice and began true and deep grief work, I was able to regain energy and enthusiasm for working with the dying and bereaved. I began a consistent exercise program, which ensured I took time for myself. I hired a personal trainer (it's a big deal for helper to ask for help!). And through grief work I choose various rituals to honor and remember those I was caring for. One of my rituals is to buy a bouquet of flowers on Friday evening. As I take each flower out of the paper wrapping, trim the stem, and place it in the vase, I think of one patient or bereaved family member and wish them well over the weekend. I intentionally place those folks in the hands of other caregivers so that I can enjoy my weekend, recharge, and be energetic when Monday arrives."

— Carol Kummet, LICSW, MTS

Questions to answer in your journal then discuss with your partner:

1. With your work and home calendars in hand, do a rough estimate of how many hours you spend in an average week on each of these activities. Be honest!
   a. Work
   b. Sleep
   c. Meals: shopping, preparation, eating, clean-up
   d. Exercise
   e. Quality time with friends and family
   f. Computer/TV/"zoning out" time
   g. Essential chores, such as laundry, errands, cleaning, etc.
   h. Spirit time
   i. Quality time with yourself that's not spent with friends/family or on exercise or spirit (such as hobbies, education, etc.)

2. Now make a pie chart. There are 168 hours in every week. On a blank page in your journal, draw a circle that takes up the entire page. The circle is the 168 hours you have to spend each week. One-quarter of the circle is 42 hours, and one-eighth of the circle is 21 hours (and so on). Draw and label pie slices that proportionately represent the activity hours you calculated above. If you want, assign each category a different color, and color it in with a colored pencil. (Alternately, you can make your pie chart on the computer, print it out and tape it into your journal.)

3. Next, make a task list and pie chart that's just for work.

4. Now meet with your responsibility partner to look over and discuss each other's pie charts. Did any of the calculations surprise you? Do any disappoint you? Which of the current pie slices do you feel best about and which do you feel worst about? Most important, how can you

reallocate your precious 168 hours a week so that overall you're spending your time more in alignment with your vision?

5. Commit to just one time adjustment for the coming week and see how it goes. Discuss the results of this adjustment next week with your responsibility partner.

A few ideas to help you embrace this week's challenge:

- *If you're not already, start taking better care of your physical self.*
  Try very hard to eat well and get adequate rest. Listen to
  what your body tells you. "Get some rest," it says. "But I
  don't have time," you reply. "I have things to do." "OK,
  then, I'll get sick so you HAVE to rest," your body says. And
  it will get sick if that's what it takes to get its needs met!
  Drink at least 5-6 glasses of water each day. Dehydration can
  compound feelings of fatigue. And don't skip exercise!
  Exercise not only provides you with more energy, it can give
  you focused thinking time. Take a 20-minute walk every day.
  Or, if that seems too much, start with a five-minute walk.

- *Explore yoga.*
  Yoga is a three-thousand-year-old practice that originated
  from Indian spiritual teachings and a mixture of physical
  postures, meditation, and deep breathing. Yoga strengthens
  you physically, emotionally, and spiritually. All yoga postures
  involve what are called *pranayamas*, or breathing purifica-
  tions, which enhance inner tranquility. Yogic breathing
  infuses your body with *prana*, or energy. If you are new to
  yoga, you will want to start with a class for beginners and
  down the line perhaps explore other types of intermediate
  and advanced practices.

- *Spend time with a companion animal.*
  We pet lovers sometimes call our pets "companion animals"
  because they are in fact our companions. Not only can pets
  be your companions, they can also help meet your need for
  physical contact. As you touch your pet, you are comforted,
  calmed, and grounded. Caring for and enjoying the company
  of animals—dogs, cats, horses, birds, deer, even fish—can
  offer an abundant supply of solace that many medical studies
  have found can help you live a longer and healthier life.
  Giving your attention to animals also requires you to slow
  down, be quiet, and become more aware of your environment. That, in turn, leads to a renewed sense of wonder and
  gratitude for the marvels that the world contains.

"When I was asked to lead a conference break-out session for professionals who care for the dying and the bereaved, I used an activity from a course I had taken at Dr. Alan Wolfelt's Center for Loss and Life Transition. Over the years, I had learned about things I might do to develop better self-care habits as I companioned bereaved children and adults. However, an activity based on a one-page handout from Dr. Wolfelt's course 'Living with Meaning and Purpose in Your Life' proved to be more helpful to me than any wisdom I had gleaned from other sources.

"Participants used the activity to identify the people involved in their personal support systems. The handout asked us to list the people we turned to for close friendship, problem-sharing, play, acceptance and approval, energizing, teaching, trying new things, professional contact, and comfort when we are hurting and want to be with someone who knows us well.

"The introductory sentence on the handout stated that we get different things from different people in our support networks, and for me, the activity helped me to broaden the way I viewed self-care. Rather than having a list of activities to incorporate into a self-care program, I now had a list of support people who had always been a natural and integral part of my self-care.

"The other professionals in my break-out session were also grateful for the awareness the activity provided. One group member realized that although he listed his wife as his support person in all nine areas, he was certain that if she took part in the activity, she would list a variety of people. He smiled and said he was going to take immediate steps to broaden his support network. Another shared that she couldn't wait to get home and arrange a get-together with friends who had always energized her. One of the younger participants said he had always thought of self-care as a more solitary endeavor.

"Often in life, simple things offer profound truths. Try this activity if you are seeking a fresh view of self-care."

— Carol Swift

Week 6: Carve Out *More* Sacred Downtime— Weekly, Monthly, Yearly

Time to just "be" seems to be in short supply these days. We are all so busy and have so many commitments that we've forgotten how to simply be present. And the proliferation of technology has only compounded this problem; at our fingertips is an infinite selection of entertainment and information.

If you're spending at least 15 minutes a day connecting with your spirit (and you'd better be, or else go back to Week 4!), you've probably begun to realize that downtime is essential to rebalancing your life and achieving your vision. Now, in addition to this daily spirit time, I want you to begin to plan for and carry out longer, regular periods of restorative time.

How much downtime is enough? That's up to you. I would suggest, however, that you set aside one full day each and every week to not work, to not engage in solitary technology activities (such as checking your e-mail or playing games online), and to spend being present to the people you love the most.

Each month, I would recommend scheduling at least one full day of away time. Leave your usual day-to-day environment and retreat to somewhere new, interesting, or relaxing. You could visit an out-of-town friend, spend a day hiking or biking, attend a seminar, take a class, etc. On at least some of these away days, go alone.

During the course of a year, I would also suggest that you schedule at least two full weeks of exile. This means leaving all your usual obligations behind (including e-mail, voicemail, etc.) and doing something that relaxes and restores you. Your budget needn't be lavish to go into exile. In fact, you can even exile yourself within the confines of your own home as long as you have the discipline to ignore your phone, computer, cleaning and other chores during the time period you designate.

Regular downtime gives you perspective and context. In taking you out of your usual world (literally or figuratively), it helps you see your own life more objectively and reminds you that you that despite all your many obligations, your world goes on just fine without you.

Questions to answer in your journal then discuss with your partner:

1. Do you observe a Sabbath? Why or why not? How do you feel about the possibility of setting aside one full day each week for nothing but relaxation, fun, and spending quality time with friends and family?

2. How often do you normally do something away from your normal life? What kinds of things do you do, and how do they make you feel? Which "away" activities within an hour or two of your home have you always wanted to try but haven't yet?

3. Describe any experiences you've had going to exile for a full week or more.

4. How do you feel about spending quality time with just yourself sometimes?

5. With your responsibility partner, discuss your answers to these questions and begin the process of carving out *and scheduling* more sacred downtime this month and this year. (Also, don't forget to review the results of the one-time scheduling adjustments that you and your partner each implemented in the week since you last met.)

A few ideas to help you embrace this week's challenge:

- *Observe the Sabbath.*
  The word "Sabbath" comes from the old Hebrew shab-bath, which literally means "to rest." Just as God rested on the 7th day of creation, Jews and Christians "keep the Sabbath" by resting and connecting with God on Saturday or Sunday, respectively. Those who strictly keep the Sabbath do no work whatsoever on their day of rest. You may choose to strictly observe a religious Sabbath as a day of renewal and connection with your Maker. Or you may choose to rest and rejuvenate one day a week as a way to embrace your spirituality.

  If you observe a Sabbath day, you will be dedicating a portion of your life to your spiritual well-being. And that, regardless of your doctrine or creed, is a healthy self-companionship practice.

- *Spend time in "thin places."*
  In the Celtic tradition, "thin places" are spots where the separation between the physical world and the spiritual world seem tenuous. They are places where the veil between Heaven and earth, between the holy and the everyday, are so thin that when we are near them, we intuitively sense the timeless, boundless spiritual world. In fact, there is a Celtic saying that heaven and earth are only three feet apart, but in the thin places that distance is even smaller. Thin places are usually outdoors, often where water and land meet or land and sky come together. You might find thin places on a riverbank, a beach, or a mountaintop. They are anywhere that fills you with awe and a sense of wonder. They are spots that refresh your spirit and make you feel closer to God. Go to a thin place to pray, to walk, or to simply sit in the presence of the holy.

- *Go on a pilgrimage.*

  Pilgrimage to a sacred place is common to all religious traditions—Christianity, Judaism, Hinduism, Islam, Native American, to name a few. The literal definition of a pilgrimage is a long journey or search, especially one of exalted purpose or moral significance. Going on a pilgrimage to a sacred place is a mark of respect and often invites spiritual renewal and inner harmony to those who make the journey. From the beginning days of the Christian church, pilgrims visited the graves of the Apostles and the martyrs. The great centers of Christian medieval pilgrimage were Jerusalem, Rome, the tomb of Saint James of Compostela in Spain, and the shrine of Saint Thomas Becket in Canterbury, England. Make plans today to go on a pilgrimage to a sacred place that connects you to your religion or spirituality.

- *Go to exile.*

  Choosing to spend time alone is an essential self-nurturing spiritual practice. It affords you the opportunity to be unaffected by other's wants and needs. It is impossible to really know yourself if you never take time to withdraw from the demands of daily living. Alone time does not mean you are being selfish. Instead, you will experience rest and renewal in ways you otherwise would not. A lack of alone time produces heightened confusion and a muting of your life force. But remember, this time of exile is not only for you. As you rest and renew, you can also better meet the needs of those who depend on you. Your human spirit is naturally compassionate, and once you feel restored, your instinct to be kind and generous to those around you will be revitalized. Within your exiled time and space will evolve the insights and blessings that come to the surface only in stillness and with time. Schedule alone time on a regular basis. Don't shut out your family and friends altogether, but do answer the call for contemplative solitude.

"Self-care is a difficult but necessary part of working with the intense emotional needs and troubles of other people. Too often, self-care takes a backseat to other priorities in life, so I consciously developed a self-care plan to make sure I tend to my needs. As a helper, I realize the importance of setting boundaries. This includes saying no when needed (without feeling guilty) and not overextending myself. I also enjoy nurturing relationships with family, friends, and myself because they are a deep source of pleasure and help me feel connected to the world. Other self-care activities include hanging out with my two dogs, engaging in prayer and meditation, maintaining a healthy lifestyle (eating, sleeping, and exercising habits), traveling, going to trainings, collaborating with colleagues, and allowing personal time for self-reflection. Despite these actions, there are times when stress gets the best of me and I am emotionally depleted. It is during these times that I turn on the television to my favorite show, grab a Diet Coke with Lime, and shut out the world for the evening or take a vacation day to do absolutely nothing."

— LeAnn Kahl

Week 7: Seek Joy

What is joy? Happiness, but elevated. Contentment to the nth degree. Delight. Bliss.

Wow. Who doesn't want to live in a state of pure joy?

For caregivers, part of the challenge of seeking joy can be letting go of the notion that having fun is "goofing off" and that work is the hard, disciplined, but necessary essence of life. If you're having fun, you must not be doing what you're supposed to be doing. But what if the disciplined seeking of joy were actually the essence of life?

This week, start paying attention to what gives you joy. It's different for everyone. For me, hiking in the mountains in my beautiful home state of Colorado is a joyful way to spend a morning. For others, gardening, singing, painting, listening to music, or baking may be joyful activities. Whatever it is for you, be present to it and seek to spend more time doing it.

Sometimes what gives you joy is something you're naturally good at. If you're a born golfer, playing golf may be a purely joyful activity. If you're not a born golfer (like me), golfing may be one of those activities that actually makes you more tense and anxious. On the other hand, you might find joy doing something that you're not particularly good at. The world might consider me a terrible poet, but if writing poetry brings me joy nonetheless, I'm meant to do it. The point is, joy-wallowing isn't about excellence-proving or approval-seeking, it's about the feeling you have when you're doing it.

Is there a difference between relaxation and joy? I think so. In America, we use the phrases "zone out" or "just veg" when we are so fatigued that we need simply to rest and recharge. Such restful activities can include watching TV, playing videogames, and surfing the web.

But joyful activities—those are the things that make us tingly happy. That make us thrilled to be alive. While restful activities may well be an appropriate part of your rebalanced week, too, I caution you against falling into the common trap of thinking that you need more couch time to correct your life-work imbalance. Zoning out may be relaxing to your body and soothing to your mind, but it does not generally connect you to your spirit. And while some spirit time is also restful (such as meditation, prayer, and certain kinds of reading, for example), often it involves engaging more actively with nature, sensory delights, and fellow human beings.

So learn to discern between joyful activities and mere distractions because this week is about beginning to discover and purposefully seek out those moments that bring you true joy. The goal is to spend more and more time in a state of bliss.

I hope that parts of your work life bring you joy, just as some of your leisure activities probably do. If so, try to figure out how to spend more of your work time doing these things and less doing tasks that bore you or you plain don't like.

Of course, ultimately the goal is to learn how to approach *everything* you do with a joyful attitude. Does anyone naturally love doing laundry or filling out paperwork, for example? Maybe not, but such necessary chores can still be approached with gratitude. Many spiritual masters believe that we can achieve this if we can learn to live from our spirit and think joyfully each and every moment. "We are shaped by our thoughts," said Buddha. "We become what we think. When the mind is pure, joy follows like a shadow that never leaves."

Questions to answer in your journal then discuss with your partner:

1. What gives you joy? Write down as many things as you can think of, big or little, including those things that gave you joy in earlier parts of your life—even when you were a child.

2. Pick the top 10 things on the joy list you just created. On a new page in your journal, write down these top 10 items. Now turn back to the pie charts you created in your journal during Week 5. How much time are you spending each week on these activities? Write the number of minutes or hours next to each item on your top 10 list.

3. Discuss your understanding of the concept of joy with your responsibility partner. Also review the time each of you allocates to joyful activities each week and how to carve out more time for them.

4. Do you have any ideas about how to make essential chores and activities more joyful? For example, you could listen to your favorite music when you clean or keep a stash of your favorite gum in your drawer at work.

A few ideas to help you embrace this week's challenge:

- *Schedule something that gives you pleasure each and every day.*
  We've acknowledged how draining it can be to companion the dying and the bereaved. To counterbalance your draining work, plan something you enjoy doing every day. Don't simply expect that it will happen—schedule it. Actually enter it on your calendar. Reading, baking, going for a walk, having lunch with a friend, playing a computer game—whatever brings you relaxation and enjoyment. Every day. Every single day.

- *Learn to live in the moment.*
  Have you ever noticed how inner peace is portrayed as a distant goal, available only to those who attain some superior knowledge of how to achieve it? Yet, a truth is that inner peace is our natural, organic state of being. Yes, sometimes inner peace can seem to be elusive, hidden by anxiety and fear that leaves you not in the here and now, but in the past or the future. But the sun shines the brightest when we are in the present moment. When the light shines, you can befriend a feeling of being whole—connected to something that extends way beyond your individual self. The here and now is the resting place for your heart and soul. You can consciously go to this place whenever you choose to. Here you can rest from the natural stress that comes with companioning the dying and the bereaved. In the present moment comes the richness of life in all of its glory. The felt experience of happiness and joy can be discovered in the present moment. You feel a kind of oneness with life that is at the very core of inner peace. To focus all of your attention in the present moment is to surrender yourself completely to whatever and whoever is with you. In experiencing this you may even feel the presence of God.

- *Know that you are loved.*

  As Jane Howard wisely observed, "Call it a clan, call it a network, call it a tribe, call it a family. Whatever you call it, whoever you are, you need one." Yes, love from family, friends, and community gives life meaning and purpose. Reflect on the people who care about you and the ways in which your life matters. Open your heart and have gratitude for those who love you. Feeling connected to people around you can be a great source of joy and a cause for celebration. When you reach out to others and they to you, you remember you are loved even during difficult days. When you consciously come together with family, friends, and community, you make the most of each moment and experience a sense of well-being and belonging in the world.

Week 8: Revise

Congratulations! You've reached the final week of the eight-week self-companioning makeover. I hope you've learned some things about yourself over the past seven weeks and have begun to make progress in rebalancing your life. Have you acknowledged that there is an imbalance? If so, good job. Have you inventoried the hurts in your life that need to be fully grieved and mourned? Excellent work. Are you taking better care of yourself physically, emotionally, cognitively, socially, and spiritually? If you can answer "yes!" to even one of those, rejoice!

But as we've said, recovering from overcaring and perfectionism in our work with the dying and the bereaved is a process, not an event, and it is almost certainly a process that you will want to repeat. The good news is that each time you step through the makeover, you're likely to gain new insights and move ever closer to your vision of an ideal life filled with joy. At the same time, you can continue to be proud, yet humbled, as you companion your fellow human beings.

This week, set aside some time to note what's working and what's not working so far in your plan to become a better self-companion. Meet with your responsibility partner and discuss how things went and whether you will continue. You might consider taking a break from the makeover process itself but pledging to continue the enhancements you've begun so far. Perhaps in six months or a year you will again be ready to reengage with the eight-week makeover process from start to finish.

Questions to answer in your journal then discuss with your partner:

1. How did the makeover process go for you? What helped? What didn't help?

2. If you step through the makeover process again, will you adjust it to better meet your unique needs? If so, how?

3. Rate your satisfaction with your work-life balance on a scale of 1 to 10, with 1 being extremely dissatisfied and 10 being extremely satisfied. Has your rating improved at all in the last eight weeks?

4. What is your dearest wish for your life in the coming year? Which steps can you commit to make to ensure this wish comes true?

A few ideas to help you embrace this week's challenge:

- *Be patient.*

  I'm sure you've realized by now that like healing in grief, recreating your life does not happen quickly. And life is, well, a lifelong journey. In our hurry-up North American culture, patience can be especially hard to come by. We have all been conditioned to believe that if we want something, we should be able to get it instantly. Yet your efforts to create the life of your dreams will not heed anyone's timetable—even your own. Be patient with yourself. Be patient with those around you. You are doing the best you can, as are they. And don't forget that practicing patience means continuing to surrender. Even as you strive to become a better self-companion, you must surrender to each day just as it is and learn to live with gratitude and joy in the moment. When you are feeling impatient, silently repeat this phrase: "Let nothing disturb thee; Let nothing dismay thee; All things pass; God never changes. Patience attains All that it strives for. He who has God finds he lacks nothing: God alone suffices."
  — Saint Teresa of Avila

- *Carry a touchstone.*

  A touchstone is a standard of quality or excellence against which you can measure other things. Let's say one of your own spiritual touchstones is "seeking peace." When you are deciding how to react in a difficult situation, you might be tempted to explode in anger. But you stop to consider your "seeking peace" touchstone and instead decide that an angry outburst would be counterproductive. You can literally carry a stone in your pocket to remind you of your spiritual touchstones, or intentions. Whenever you're feeling fatigue in your work or struggling with a thought or feeling, put your hand in your pocket and rub your touchstone. The stone's smooth surface and the rubbing motion will help center you and return you to your place of spiritual intention.

- *Look for the surprises and gifts in your day.*
  Stop reading this and look around you, where you are right this moment. Look at the same things you see each day, but through a different set of eyes. What are you grateful for that is within your view? See it with awe. Look at the face of someone you love and rejoice that he is in your life. Whatever comes into your path today, consider it a gift. Take a moment to receive the gift and appreciate the giver. Embrace the warm feelings that come from being connected, from the link to gratefulness. Say "yes" and "thank you." As Bill Keane said, "Yesterday's the past, tomorrow's the future, but today is a gift. That's why it's called the present."

A Final Word

In the hundreds of training seminars I have led over the past 30 years, I have been privileged to meet thousands of caregivers to the dying and the bereaved from all around the world. What a special group you are. To a one, you are kind, compassionate, enthusiastic givers. Day in and day out, you give of yourselves to help your fellow human beings, and in doing so, you are, as Gandhi challenged, "the change you want to see in the world." I am so honored to count so many of you among my friends.

At the same time, I know that quite a number of you are dealing with work-life imbalances that are affecting not only your quality of life but also the quality of life of the people around you. It doesn't have to be so! I wrote this book to help you as you have helped so many others.

This book is my thank you to you. Please accept it and take it to heart in the spirit in which it is given—from an admirer who understands how challenging your work is and who wants only the best for you. Because that is what you deserve.

I would also like to invite you to send me your thoughts about and experiences with self-companionship for caregivers to the dying and the bereaved. Please e-mail me at DrWolfelt@centerforloss.com.

Bless you. If I have not yet been fortunate enough to meet you, I hope we cross paths one day.

A Self-Companionship Manifesto for Caregivers to the Dying and the Bereaved

We who care for the dying and the bereaved have a wondrous opportunity: to help others embrace and grow through grief—and to lead fuller, more deeply-lived lives ourselves because of this important ministry.

But our work is draining—physically, emotionally and spiritually. We must first care for ourselves if we want to care well for others. This manifesto is intended to empower you to practice good self-companionship.

1. *I deserve to lead a joyful, whole life.* No matter how much I love and value my work, my life is multi-faceted. My family, my friends, my other interests, and my spirituality also deserve my time and attention. I deserve my time and attention.

2. *My work does not define me.* I am a unique, worthy person outside my work life. While relationships can help me feel good about myself, they are not what is inside me. Sometimes I need to stop "doing" and instead focus on simply "being."

3. *I am not the only one who can help bereaved people.* When I feel indispensable, I tend to ignore my own needs. There are many talented caregivers in my community who can also help the bereaved.

4. *I must develop healthy eating, sleeping, and exercise patterns.* I am aware of the importance of these things for those I help, but I may neglect them myself. A well-

balanced diet, adequate sleep, and regular exercise allow me to be the best I can be.

5. *If I've been overinvolved in my caregiving for too long, I may have forgotten how to take care of myself.* I may need to rediscover ways of caring for and nurturing myself. I may need to relearn how to explore my own feelings instead of focusing on everybody else's.

6. *I must maintain boundaries in my helping relationships.* As a caregiver, I cannot avoid getting emotionally involved with bereaved people. Nor would I want to. Active empathy allows me to be a good companion to them. However, I must remember I am responsible *to* others, not *for* others.

7. *I am not perfect and I must not expect myself to be.* I often wish my helping efforts were always successful. But even when I offer compassionate, "on-target" help, the recipient of that help isn't always prepared to use it. And when I do make mistakes, I should see them as an integral part of learning and growth, not as measurements of my self-worth.

8. *I must practice effective time-management skills.* I must set practical goals for how I spend my time. I must also remember Pareto's principle: twenty percent of what I do nets eighty percent of my results.

9. *I must also practice setting limits and alleviating stresses I can do something about.* I must work to achieve a clear sense of expectations and set realistic deadlines. I should enjoy what I do accomplish in helping others but shouldn't berate myself for what is beyond me.

10. *I must listen to my inner voice.* As a caregiver to the bereaved, I will at times become grief overloaded. When my inner voice begins to whisper its fatigue, I must listen carefully and allow myself some grief down-time.

11. *I should express the personal me in both my work and play.* I shouldn't be afraid to demonstrate my unique talents and abilities. I must also make time each day to remind myself of what is important to me. If I only had three months to live, what would I do?

12. *I am a spiritual being.* I must spend alone time focusing on self-understanding and self-love. To be present to those I work with and to learn from those I companion, I must appreciate the beauty of life and living. I must renew my spirit.

Beautiful color wallet cards of the Caregiver's Self-Care Manifesto are available from Companion Press for $15.00 for a packet of 50. Visit www.centerforloss.com to order.

ALSO BY DR. ALAN D. WOLFELT

Companioning the Bereaved
A Soulful Guide for Caregivers

This book by one of North America's most respected grief educators presents a model for grief counseling based on his "companioning" principles.

For many mental healthcare providers, grief in contemporary society has been medicalized—perceived as if it were an illness that with proper assessment, diagnosis, and treatment could be cured.

Dr. Wolfelt explains that our modern understanding of grief all too often conveys that at bereavement's "end" the mourner has completed a series of tasks, extinguished pain, and established new relationships. Our psychological models emphasize "recovery" or "resolution" in grief, suggesting a return to "normalcy."

By contrast, this book advocates a model of "companioning" the bereaved, acknowledging that grief forever changes or transforms the mourner's world view. Companioning is not about assessing, analyzing, fixing, or resolving another's grief. Instead, it is about being totally present to the mourner, even being a temporary guardian of his soul. The companioning model is grounded in a "teach me" perspective.

"This outstanding book should be required reading for each and every grief provider. Dr. Wolfelt's philosophy and practice of caregiving helps us understand we don't need to be joined at the head with the mourner, we need to be joined at the heart." — grief counselor

ISBN 978-1-879651-41-8 • 191 pages • hardcover • $29.95

Companion
PRESS

All Dr. Wolfelt's publications can be ordered by mail from:
Companion Press
3735 Broken Bow Road
Fort Collins, CO 80526
(970) 226-6050
www.centerforloss.com

ALSO BY DR. ALAN D. WOLFELT

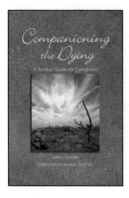

Companioning the Dying
A Soulful Guide for Caregivers

by Greg Yoder
Foreword by Alan D. Wolfelt, Ph.D.

Based on the assumption that all dying experiences belong not to the caregivers but to those who are dying—and that there is no such thing as a "good death" or a "bad death"—*Companioning the Dying* helps readers bring a respectful, nonjudgmental presence to the dying while liberating them from self-imposed or popular expectations to say or do the right thing.

Written with candor and wit by hospice counselor Greg Yoder (who has companioned several hundred dying people and their families), *Companioning the Dying* exudes a compassion and a clarity that can only come from intimate work with the dying. The book teaches through real-life stories that will resonate with both experienced clinical professionals as well as laypeople in the throes of caring for a dying loved one.

ISBN 978-1-61722-149-1 • 148 pages • softcover • $19.95

Companion

All Dr. Wolfelt's publications can be ordered by mail from:
Companion Press
3735 Broken Bow Road
Fort Collins, CO 80526
(970) 226-6050
www.centerforloss.com

ALSO BY DR. ALAN D. WOLFELT

Companioning the Grieving Child

A Soulful Guide for Caregivers

Renowned author and educator Dr. Alan Wolfelt redefines the role of the grief counselor in this guide for caregivers to grieving children. Providing a viable alternative to the limitations of the medical establishment's model for companioning the bereaved, Dr. Wolfelt encourages counselors and other caregivers to aspire to a more compassionate philosophy in which the child is the expert of his or her grief—not the counselor or caregiver. The approach outlined in the book argues against treating grief as an illness to be diagnosed and treated but rather for acknowledging it as an experience that forever changes a child's worldview. By promoting careful listening and observation, this guide shows caregivers, family members, teachers, and others how to support grieving children and help them grow into healthy adults.

ISBN 978-1-61722-158-3 • 160 pages • hardcover • $29.95

Companion
PRESS

All Dr. Wolfelt's publications can be ordered by mail from:
Companion Press
3735 Broken Bow Road
Fort Collins, CO 80526
(970) 226-6050
www.centerforloss.com

To contact Dr. Wolfelt about speaking engagements or training opportunities at his Center for Loss and Life Transition, email him at DrWolfelt@centerforloss.com.